table of
CONTE

FEATURES

64

58

80

COVER PHOTO: *Joyelle West*
STYLIST: *Karin Lidbeck-Brent*
DESIGNER: *Jenn Sanborn*

table of CONTENTS

22

DEPARTMENTS

FOR EDITORIAL QUESTIONS, EMAIL BEAUTIFULKITCHENS@MEREDITH.COM
OR WRITE US AT *BEAUTIFUL KITCHENS & BATHS,*
PREMIUM PUBLISHING,
1716 LOCUST ST., DES MOINES, IA 50309-3023

I REMEMBER MY MOTHER CALLING ME IN A PANIC A FEW YEARS AGO. Her kitchen remodeling project was about to get under way and she hadn't yet made up her mind about several key elements of the design. Should she include an island? Should she opt for a simple granite backsplash or the glass mosaic tile that had caught her eye in the showroom? Should she include custom pullout baskets for veggies in the base cabinets? Should she conceal the dishwasher behind a cabinetry panel?

I had my own set of answers based on my experience editing this magazine and my personal preferences, but this new kitchen wasn't going to be my kitchen. I knew that the only guarantee of success was for my mom to answer her own questions. But she was stuck! So I suggested that she close her eyes and picture her dream kitchen. Forget the cost—at least for now—and just imagine coming home at five o'clock, pouring a glass of wine, and setting it on the counter. What is that countertop made of? As dinner simmers on the cooktop, what does she see in front of her? Is the backsplash eye-catching or subdued? Where are her guests sitting?

The picture my mother drew was simple but stunning: creamy cabinets with bronze knobs, lots of hidden storage compartments, a peninsula where friends could pull up a chair, and a butcher-block-topped island just big enough to function as a de facto cutting board. And that's the kitchen she created. She said a big yes to the veggie baskets (and loves them). She tucked the dishwasher behind panels (no fingerprints!). And she took a chance on the backsplash tile, choosing colorful glass over stone. It is her favorite feature of the kitchen and offers a great lesson to anyone who might be hemming and hawing over a design decision: If something makes you smile once, it is likely to do so again.

Samantha

SAMANTHA HART
Editor, *Beautiful Kitchens & Baths™*

Let's Talk About SUSTAINABILITY

Reduce water and energy consumption, cut costs, and minimize waste with these sustainable and stylish products.

CULPRIT

Dishwasher

CAN CAUSE WATER WASTE AND EXCESSIVE ENERGY USE

Solution:

ENERGY STAR–RATED DISHWASHER

A dishwasher requires less water than washing by hand. Save even more water with one that has soil sensors to regulate water and electricity use during cycles. **Bosch 500 Series 24 in. Stainless Steel Top Control Tall Tub Pocket Handle Dishwasher with Stainless Steel Tub, AutoAir, 44dBA, $1,099;** *bosch-home.com*

CULPRIT

Kitchen Faucet

CAN CAUSE WATER WASTE

Solution:

LOW-FLOW FAUCET

To determine whether a faucet is water-efficient, look for a WaterSense label, which means the faucet can use a maximum of 1.5 gallons per minute, reducing flow and thus how much water is used. **Fluted Single-Handle Pull-Down Kitchen Faucet in Matte Black, $264;** *peerlessfaucet.com*

CULPRIT

Cooking Appliance

CAN CAUSE ENERGY WASTE

Solution:

INDUCTION COOKING

Electromagnetic energy turns the cookware itself into the heat source, meaning less heat loss. This makes induction cooktops more energy-efficient than electric or gas. Bonus: You can't burn yourself! **Smeg SPR30UIMX, $4,399;** *smeg.com*

MINDFUL MATERIALS

- ***Buy local.*** Items made near you have a smaller carbon footprint. (They don't have to travel far to get to you.) Purchasing local products also supports your local economy.
- ***Choose sustainability-focused brands.*** Purchase home design products from companies that prioritize renewable energy, recycling, and carbon-neutral manufacturing processes.
- ***Reuse salvaged materials where you can.*** When renovating your kitchen or bath, see what can be repurposed in the new design. Repaint dated cabinetry or refinish flooring for a fresh look without buying new. Vintage fixtures and salvaged materials, such as reclaimed wood, add character, reduce costs, and promote sustainability.

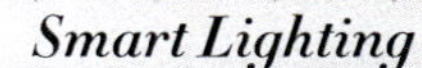

Smart Lighting

To lower the power consumption of lighting, stick to LED bulbs, which come in a range of hues and now offer smart features such as app-controlled settings. Install large low-E glass doors and windows to get natural light without all of the heat.

PHOTO Brie Williams DESIGNER Cortney Bishop

CULPRIT

Bath Faucet

CAN CAUSE WATER WASTE

Solution:

SPLASH-REDUCING FAUCET

Just like in the kitchen, fixtures in the bath should be water-efficient. Beyond the WaterSense label, look for splash-resistant designs to prevent water pooling atop counters. **Trinsic Two Handle Widespread Bathroom Faucet in Champagne Bronze, $425;** *deltafaucet.com*

CULPRIT

Showerhead

CAN CAUSE WATER WASTE

Solution:

LOW-FLOW DESIGN

With a max emittance of 1.75 gallons per minute, these showerheads keep water usage minimal. **Kohler Forté 1.75 GPM multifunction showerhead with Katalyst air-induction technology, $148;** *kohler.com*

CULPRIT

Bathtub

CAN BE CONSTRUCTED WITH HARMFUL MATERIALS

Solution:

ECO-FRIENDLY BATHTUB

Showering uses less water than a bathtub, but if you can't resist a good long soak, consider a tub made of sustainable materials. **Avalon 62 in Slate 62-Inch NativeStone Freestanding Soaking Tub, $8,990;** *nativetrails.com*

PHOTO Ryann Ford DESIGNER Emily Seiders

Water-Saving Idea

Dual-flush toilets cost a little more upfront, but the reduced water usage saves money over time.

Which surface is right for you?

When selecting sustainable materials for countertops, flooring, tub surrounds, or wall tile, it's a give and take.

Hybrid or Engineered Stone

PRO: Engineered surfaces give the look of natural stone with customized designs, but unlike stone, they are stain- and scratch-resistant and require little maintenance. For example, Consentino's Silestone is a blend of quartz and recycled materials (including glass) produced using the brand's zero-waste manufacturing process, Hybriq.
CON: Because of the combination of its materials, manufactured surfaces are not as resistant to heat as natural stone.

Porcelain Tile

PRO: In addition to being nonporous and resistant to heat, water, and stains, this type of ceramic tile has a long lifespan and is recyclable.
CON: Porcelain is more expensive than other tiles.

Natural Stone

PRO: Materials like quartzite, marble, and granite are naturally occurring and recyclable, and have longevity and versatility.
CON: The extraction, production process, and transportation of natural stone require a lot of energy, water, and fuel consumption.

Natural Wood

PRO: Natural and renewable, wood can be even more eco-friendly if you buy local, salvaged, or from a manufacturer who sources lumber responsibly with minimal environmental impact.
CON: For countertops and flooring, wood can be tricky as it's temperature-sensitive and hard to maintain.

Engineered Wood

PRO: Manufactured wood, from brands such as Duchateau, has the appearance of natural wood with less upkeep. Production of the planks uses less of a tree than is required for solid hardwoods and sometimes includes recycled or leftover wood.
CON: The planks are not 100-percent natural, but rather comprise different materials adhered together (although the blend is seamless).

1

Add glass fronts to some of the room's cabinetry to create a focal point, like Robinn and Doug McAllister did in their home to display Robinn's extensive ironstone collection.

BEHIND THE SCENES

Auxiliary spaces hide the dirty work, house an arsenal of products, and help keep the rest of the home looking its best. Take a cue from these ultra-functional rooms to make the most of yours.

PRODUCER *Samantha Stevenson*

2 A butler's pantry doesn't need to have a large footprint; sometimes a small corner sink is all you need. This nook from designer Suzanne Kasler gets it just right. ▪3 As seen with this chef-approved pantry by designer Heidi Arwine, open shelving provides quick and easy access to kitchen essentials. ▪4 A spacious mudroom, like this one in Cale and Ashley Rice's home, is an efficient spot for cleanup upon entering the house—and before stepping foot (or paw) into the main rooms. Outfit the utility room with a pet bathing station, a laundry sink, and ample cabinetry. Add decorative touches such as artwork to make the space as pretty as it is practical.

PHOTOS John Granen (opposite), Eric Piasecki (top left), Lindsay Salazar (top right), Jay Wilde (bottom)

5

A library ladder adds classic charm and ensures you can reach the highest shelves of a storage space, like in this blue-and-purple pantry by designer Benjamin Johnston.

6

7

8

9

PHOTOS Julie Soefer (opposite), Tria Giovan (top left), Nathan Schroder (top right), Kerry Kirk (bottom left), Adam Albright (bottom right)

6 If you find yourself with extra storage in a mudroom or utility space, consider creating a lounging spot for your pets (like this one by SKM Design) to avoid bulky kennels. • 7 Lean into styles perhaps too daring for larger rooms in the home. Interior designers Kimberly Rasmussen and Elizabeth Wixom Johnsen used deep green, a soapstone sink, and toile Roman shades to give this pantry a European look. • 8 Take a cue from this laundry room by designer Laurin White and select a muted paint color and a mix of antiques, prints, and botanicals to soften a hard-working space's edges. • 9 A bright and vibrant color brings energy to this cleanup space by designer Elizabeth Darth of Martha O'Hara Interiors. Position the sink beneath a window to cheer up chores.

THIS PHOTO: Designer Caren Rideau incorporates furniturelike cabinetry to store essential dishware and cooking utensils. A glass-front hutch puts wooden pieces on display.

Host With the Most

There are three things designer Caren Rideau enjoys most: cooking, wine, and throwing a good dinner party. A well-zoned kitchen (and hardworking secondary spaces), she says, can make entertaining feel effortless.

WRITER *Samantha Stevenson*

How do you design kitchens with both entertaining and cooking in mind?

I love to cook, and it's always been important to me and a part of my culture. Because I understand cooking and how one might cook, it's easy for me to set up a kitchen as I am doing the design work. If you do casual entertaining or if you do formal entertaining, you have to consider what your needs are and what needs to be placed where. When entertaining, I always want to be a part of the group. I don't like to separate myself. To achieve that, everything I am preparing has to be easy, like a cheese plate or grilling. It's all about the presentation and making everyone feel a part of it.

How does the kitchen's layout play a role in that togetherness?

I look at how the kitchen relates to the sitting areas. I don't mind a prep sink where you are washing produce for cooking, but I'm not so fond of a cleanup sink in the island. You are mixing the task of a cleanup with the entertaining. I think of the kitchen layout in different segments. I define a cooking area, a cleanup area, and a prep space. Designating those spaces makes it easier for more than one person to be in the kitchen and not be in each other's way.

How do auxiliary spaces, such as a scullery or butler's pantry, make the main kitchen more functional?

I love those spaces. If I can, I incorporate those rooms into my kitchens as a transition area from the dining room to the kitchen or a place to house extra dishes, but not everyone has the space for that. An alternative is a smaller unit room for small appliances and prep tools that usually crowd the countertops.

How can homeowners who don't have those additional rooms create storage?

It's nice to have a piece of furniture, out of the cook's path, where dishes and flatware can be housed. There's nothing worse than when you're cooking and someone's coming in to get a plate. In cabinets close to the table, I always put in drawers that are set up for everyday flatware and dishes. If you don't have room to put your plates in the upper cabinets, you can set up drawers that will house them.

What are your tips for preparing to host a gathering?

I would say start with very simple things. Everything doesn't have to match: You can have eight different plates that are just plates you love. Set a table that makes the guests feel special. It's all about the joy of being with family and friends and how that joy transfers to the table.

IN HER FIRST BOOK, *Caren Rideau: Kitchen Designer, Vintner, Entertaining at Home* (2022; Pointed Leaf Press), the designer's passions influence her designs—with go-to recipes, wine pairings, and colorful kitchens to boot.

PHOTO *Meghan Beierle-O'Brien (opposite)*

Coffee Table Pick ▸
See more in designer Lauren Liess' *Down to Earth: Laid-Back Interiors for Modern Living* (2019; Abrams Books).

GET THE LOOK

Perhaps your taste is contemporary, rustic, or somewhere in between. Take your pick, then ace the style with these key items.

PRODUCER *Pamela Porter*

Earthy Modern

In a New Light

Midcentury meets industrial-cool as the wrought-iron shades of this linear light flaunt an interior finish of gold leaf. **9841 Culpepper Rectangular Chandelier ($2,120). Currey and Company;** *curreyandcompany.com*

Rock Solid

This contemporary sculptural hardware features an organic, polished-stonelike form that gives an unexpected touch to cabinets. Both timeless and sophisticated, this gem is available in a dozen finishes. **Madeline Cabinet Knob in White Bronze ($59). Rocky Mountain Hardware;** *rockymountainhardware.com*

Wall Power

Crafted by Amish artisans, these shelves display all the character you'd expect to find from decades-old barnwood. Choose from six lengths, two depths, and three finishes. **Set of Two Reclaimed Barn Wood Accent Shelves with Full Accent Brackets size 36x7-inch ($158.60). Urban Legacy;** *urbanlegacy.us*

Vintage-Style Vessel

Crafted by hand of earthenware with a glazed black finish and rustic patina, this multihandle vase creates an effortless, collected style. The urn-shape treasure is watertight and lead- and latex-free. **Joshua Handcrafted Ceramic Vase in Large ($99). Pottery Barn;** *potterybarn.com*

Keep Your Cool

A revolutionary design means the flat-panel doors are customizable and changeable in a variety of colors and finishes. Enjoy Wi-Fi connectivity, a dual icemaker, and full or counter depth. **Bespoke 3-Door Full-Depth French Door Refrigerator with Beverage Center in Charcoal Glass ($3,299). Samsung;** *samsung.com*

Go With the Grain

Artisan-crafted from American white oak, this cabinet exhibits a heroic scale with a humble silhouette. Crisp angles and spare design enhance the wood's distinct texture and imperfections to achieve a rustic-modern form. **Davos Oak Cabinet in Aged Oak ($4,895; member price $3,671). Restoration Hardware;** *restorationhardware.com*

Seat Savvy

This inviting leather seat floats on a welded-iron frame that gently flexes for greater comfort. Full-grain, full-aniline-dyed leather exhibits natural variations in color and texture and develops a rich burnished patina over time. **Classic Cantilever Leather Counter Stool in Churchfield Camel ($599). Pottery Barn;** *potterybarn.com*

Filled to the Brim

The perfect blend of style and function, this wall-mount pot filler flaunts modest design and a space-saving folding arm that retracts completely when not in use. **Modern Matte Black Pot Filler Kitchen Faucet ($1,323). Moen;** *moen.com*

PHOTO *Helen Norman* DESIGNER *Lauren Liess*

French Renaissance

Full Bloom

Woven with performance fibers and inspired by antique block prints, this fabric is stain-resistant, colorfast, and ideal for a window treatment or seat cushion. S&L Performance Deauville in Coastal Blue ($78 per yard). Serena & Lily; *serenaandlily.com*

Light the Way

Modest curves, an aged-gold finish, and crystal accents give this chandelier graceful, heirloom-status presence without overdoing it. The design is available in three sizes to suit any space. Kinsale Medium Chandelier in Antique Gild ($2,380). Circa Lighting; *circalighting.com*

In Living Color

This professional-grade range features ultra-high-efficiency smart gas-burner technology and a choice of customizable or preset configurations. Le Provençal 1600 Le Classique Range in London Blue Matte with Combination Polished Chrome and Burnished Brass (contact for pricing). L'Atelier Paris; *latelierparis.com*

In the Groove

With a stepped-bevel cut on its raised-center panel, this sophisticated cabinet door is available in a variety of fine finishes. The full-overlay profile exudes elegance, depth, and old-world charm. Raised Panel 17 Door in Serenity (contact for pricing). KraftMaid; *kraftmaid.com*

Fine Dining

This triple-step-edge table has a substantial four-sided baluster-shape base and certainly leaves a lasting impression. Available in two hand-applied finishes. Andrews Pedestal Dining Table 48-inch in Washed Walnut ($2,599). Ballard Designs; *ballarddesigns.com*

Cooking Class

This porcelain enamel cast-iron cookware is crafted by French artisans and features a Dutch oven, saucepan, and highly rated skillet. Pick one of several colors, and plan to use the set for years to come. Le Creuset Signature 5-Piece Cookware Set in Ocean ($835). Williams Sonoma; *williams-sonoma.com*

Walk this Way

An aged-patina finish, metallic shimmer, and subtle relief texture define this Spanish-made porcelain tile. Angela Harris Flatiron Matte Porcelain 24x48-inch Tile in White ($7.95 per square foot). Tilebar; *tilebar.com*

A Little Gem

Inspired by Golden Age design, this barbed quatrefoil knob comes in 12 high-end finishes to add elegant detail to cabinets. 1½-inch Quatrafoil Cabinet Knob in Silicone Bronze Light ($53). Rocky Mountain Hardware; *rockymountainhardware.com*

PHOTO *Brie Williams* DESIGNER *Alix Rico*

Elevated Farmhouse

Hold Your Horses ▸

This curated collection of equestrian prints is reproduced from original late-1800s portraits using a giclee process on archival-quality cotton paper. Choose from three sizes with a white border for framing. **Set of Four Vintage Horse Portraits 5x7-inch ($65). Hart Equestrian;** ***hartequestrian.com***

Perfectly Imperfect

Transform a kitchen with authentic Moroccan-style terra-cotta zellige tiles and celebrate the inherent irregularities, color variations, and signature flaws of the handcrafted beauties. **Zellige Tile in Weathered White 4x4-inch ($19.95 per square foot).**

◂ **Clé Tile;** ***cletile.com***

PHOTO *John Granen* DESIGNER *Krissy Peterson*

What's Beautiful

Front and Center

Streamlined and versatile, this apron-front sink features a horizontal ridge pattern on the front and a low barrier inside to divide two sink compartments. Crafted from enameled cast iron, the sink resists chipping, cracking, and burning for years of beauty and reliable performance. **Whitehaven Hayridge Smart Divide 35-11/16-inch Undermount Double-Bowl Farmhouse Kitchen Sink in White ($1,988). Kohler;** ***kohler.com***

Golden Age

This gooseneck faucet marries modern lines with farmhouse charm. A 360-degree swivel spout and high arch mean maximum maneuverability and clearance. Choose from five finishes. **2-Handle Port Haven Faucet in Brushed Gold ($974). Pfister Faucets;** ***pfisterfaucets.com***

Industrial Revolution

Add this Thomas O'Brien design to keep an upscale farmhouse from appearing too glam. A pair or trio of these 21-inch-wide pendants will add a rustic touch above any island. **Eugene Large Pedant Light in Hand-Rubbed Bronze ($819). Circa Lighting;** ***circalighting.com***

Three's a Charm

Available individually or as a set, these cabinets work overtime to display, store and serve. Adjustable shelves with plate grooves, drawers, dividers, and a marble slab are just a few noteworthy features. **Paulette Server set of 3 ($6,597). Ballard Designs;** ***ballarddesigns.com***

On Island Time

Designed by Amber Lewis, this 48x84-inch rustic pine wood island offers ample storage and work space for busy kitchens. Metal hardware pulls and natural wood-grain variations and texture emphasize the primitive design. **Garvey Kitchen Island ($2,798). Anthropologie;** ***anthropologie.com***

Pretty Pastels

Vintage-inspired floral motifs, a soft color palette, and plush fibers make this affordable beauty a romantic addition to any space. **Eden Mughal Rose Blush Printed Rug ($50–$530). Rifle Paper Co. x Loloi Rugs;** ***riflepaperco.com***

30 MOST INNOVATIVE PRODUCTS 2023

Upgrading your kitchen or bath? Consider these award-winning products, which pair state-of-the-art features with high style.

WRITER *Samantha Stevenson*

1

Lights Up
This wave-inspired light fixture is extra stylish with its ceramic ruffles. The design can be a flush mount or semi-flush mount. Maisie Pendant, Megan Molten X Mitzi Tastemakers Collection (starting at $198). Hudson Valley; *hudsonvalleylighting.hvlgroup.com*

2

Sage Style
True Residential's new color series—powder-coated in-house—offers a subtle nod to nature and brings a refreshing, peaceful look to any kitchen. Sage finish (pricing varies). True Residential; *true-residential.com*

3

Sommelier's Dream
Preserve and store up to four bottles of wine with two customizable temperature zones (reds and whites can be chilled at their recommended temps). Bottles stay fresh for up to 60 days. 24-Inch Built-In Wine Dispenser ($5,999). Dacor; *dacor.com*

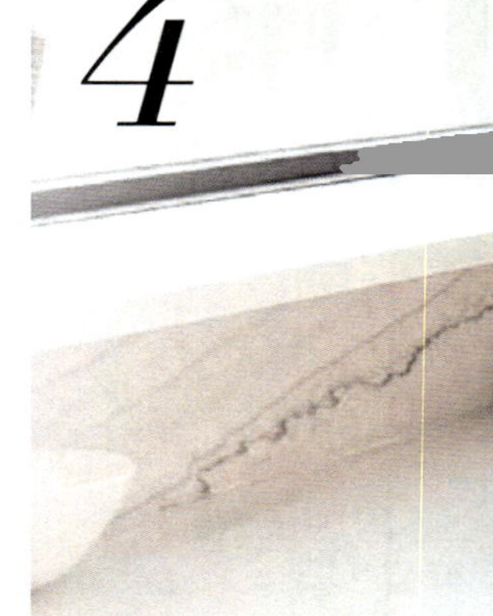

4

Hands Free
Messy hands? No problem. Control the water temperature and flow of this touchless faucet using hand motions, the Moen Smart App, or a digital voice assistant like Amazon's Alexa. Smart Faucet with Motion Control ($675). Moen; *moen.com*

5

Keep It Cool

This refrigerator's features include an intelligent cooling system, a NASA-inspired air purification system that cleans every 20 minutes, and LED lighting that reduces shadows and adjusts to light—all hidden behind panels. Sub-Zero Designer Series Refrigeration (starting at $8,205). Sub-Zero Group; *subzero-wolf.com*

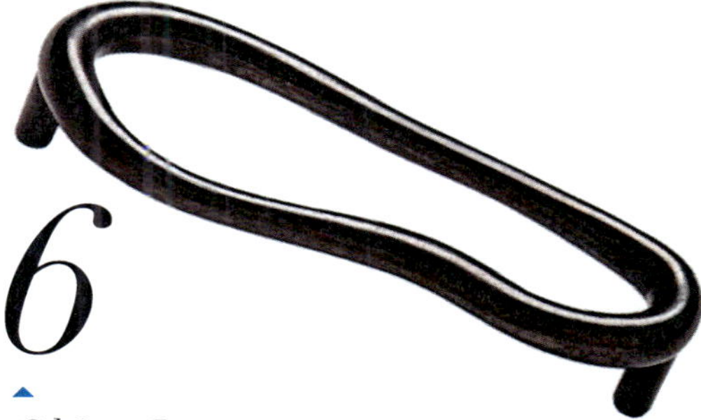

6

Object Lesson

Designed by an architecture firm, this collection features hand-crafted bronze pulls that fit any style cabinetry. Ophelia Cabinet Pulls ($55–$70). Rocky Mountain Hardware; *rockymountainhardware.com*

7

On the Surface

Part of a collaboration with interior designer Nina Magnon, these marble-inspired slabs—available in eight colors—are made from a blend of raw materials, porcelain, and glass. Dekton Onirika (pricing available upon request). Cosentino; *cosentino.com*

8

Act Naturally

This wood reproduction has the unfinished look and tactile feel of real wood with an anti-fingerprint and light- and water-resistant design. Natura 744 (pricing available upon request). Nobilia; *nobilia.de*

9

Lightened Load

This smart washer and dryer (which learns your care preferences) comes in four finishes and can be stowed atop matching risers for extra storage (as seen here) or stacked in smaller spaces. **Bespoke AI Laundry ($999–$2,998). Samsung;** ***samsung.com***

10

Compliments to the Chef

Sleek in design, this induction cooktop doesn't need overhead ventilation (a.k.a. place it anywhere!); its nine fan speeds seamlessly extract cooking odors. **36-Inch Induction Cooktop with Integrated Ventilation ($5,999). Fisher & Paykel;** ***fisherpaykel.com***

11

Light the Way

This sensor switch (installed behind cabinetry) detects motion, turning on out-of-sight lights as you enter. **Doppler Motion Sensor Switch ($43). Task Lighting and Power;** ***hardwareresources.com***

Golden Age

This two-handle tub filler has a linear gooseneck spout and lever handles and can fill a tub at a rate of 14–18 gallons per minute. **Classic Freestanding Tub Faucet (pricing varies). Franz Viegener;** ***franzviegener.com***

13

12

Set the Table

This Rosso Lepanto marble worktop is raised off eucalyptus wood cabinetry, appearing to float. A cooking zone is integrated into the stone. **+Modo (pricing available upon request). Poggenpohl;** ***poggenpohl.com***

14

Sweet Serenity

Inspired by traditional Japanese bathing and tea culture, designer Sebastian Herkner developed this collection of soft-silhouette tubs to offer an immersive feeling of tranquility. **Zencha Freestanding Bathtub (starting at $7,120). Duravit;** ***duravit.us***

15

Dine Alfresco

Enhance your outdoor kitchen with this stylish collection of stainless-steel appliances. **Elements Collection (pricing varies).** Belgard; *belgard.com*

16

Gem of a Find

This hardware collaboration with designer Barrie Benson pairs flair with function for one-of-a-kind looks. **McCoy Knobs and Pulls ($79–$140).** Modern Matter; *modern-matter.com*

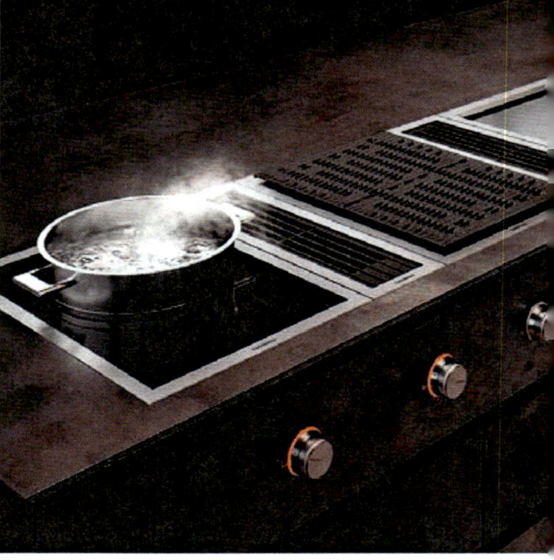

17

Fan Club ▸

Designed to fit flush against a cooktop, this low-noise ventilation system has a remote fan unit and automatic power adjustment to efficiently remove odors and vapors. **400 Series Vario Downdraft Ventilation System ($1,649). Gaggenau;** ***gaggenau.com***

18

Top Gear

Give your bath an industrial edge with the gearlike handles of this faucet, designed in collaboration with architect Barry Goralnick. **The James Collection ($1,427). Watermark Designs;** ***watermark-designs.com***

19

Vanity Flair

This stylish floating vanity is handcrafted from reclaimed oak stave weathered from months of soaking in wine. **Vintner's Floating Vanity with Drawer ($2,990). Native Trails;** ***nativetrailshome.com***

20

Window Shopping

Allow more light into your house with this hidden screen which moves with the window's sash, appearing when the window is open and concealed when it's shut. **Integrated Rohlscreen retractable screen (pricing available upon request). Pella;** ***pella.com***

21

Statement Maker

This sleek showerhead comes in several rich finishes and boasts a range of sprays, including massage options. Complete the look with a matching handshower and body sprayer to turn your bath into the ultimate retreat. **The Statement Showering Collection ($110–$1,998). Kohler;** *kohler.com*

22

Subtle Movement

A collaboration with fashion designer Guillermo Mariotto, this chiaroscuro-inspired floor and wall covering plays with light and shadows to mimic billowing fabric. **Luce (pricing available upon request). Iris Ceramica Group;** *irisceramica.com*

23

Magic Mix

Baking can be a piece of cake with a mixer, which, thanks to auto-sense technology, actively optimizes mixing and whipping to nail the most tricky of recipes. **GE Smart Stand Mixer with Auto Sense ($999). GE Profile;** *ge.com*

24

Let it Slide

Divvy up a bath or walk-in closet with a floor-to-ceiling sliding panel. Custom-made for its space, the partition adds organic architectural detail. **Spazio wall system (pricing varies). Rimadesio;** ***rimadesio.it***

25

Hanging Out

Mounted from the ceiling, this ultra-modern faucet has a striking look and can be controlled wirelessly or by a water-resistant puck. With various spray options and extra mobility, dishes might just become less of a chore. **Purist Suspend Kitchen Faucet ($4,860). Kohler;** ***kohler.com***

26

Wash Up

Sustainable engineered stone and a scratch- and stain-resistant surface makes this sink an ideal companion for a modern bath. **Silestone Evita Sink (pricing available upon request). Cosentino;** ***cosentino.com***

27

Designer's Eye

Floor-to-ceiling, 96-inch refrigeration panels, matching ventilation hood, and leather-wrapped hardware are among the dazzling details of these jewelry-inspired custom appliances. **Monogram Designer Collection x Richard Anuszkiewicz (starts at $20,000). Monogram;** ***monogram.com***

28 *Pizza Party*

This freestanding pizza oven's elegant design rivals its superior function—dual gas burners consistently deliver a crisp pizza crust without burning the cheese. Delta Heat Pizza Oven ($6,476–$6,685), Dometic Delta Heat; *deltaheat.com*

29 *Bon Appétit*

Upgrade your chef skills (and simplify cooking) with faster boiling times, a touch screen, multirack cooking, Gourmet Mode with 50 presets, and Wi-Fi ability to control from a phone. Dinner is (more easily) served! Wolf Induction Range (starting at $8,770). Sub-Zero Group; *subzero-wolf.com*

30 *In Bloom*

Enter a state of tranquility with this artsy mosaic tile. With soft pink and white blossoms against a light-blue backdrop, the Japanese Cherry Blossom mural might as well be in a gallery. Cherry Blossom in Cabana (pricing available upon request). Artaic; *artaic.com*

Ready for a CLOSE-UP

A once cramped and gloomy galley kitchen is now wide open for culinary adventures.

WRITER Laura Kostelny
PHOTOS Edmund Barr
FIELD EDITOR Karen Reinecke

LEFT: Open shelving adds dimension to the space. "Once I defined how the room would lay out, I wanted to add another focal point," designer Melissa Prevost says. "I don't love cabinets that turn corners, so we flanked the window with shelves instead."

THIS PHOTO: Designer Melissa Prevost brought a sense of moodiness to this California kitchen by mixing natural white oak with midnight blue paint on the cabinets. She further leaned into contrast with black honed-granite countertops along the room's perimeter paired with a crisp white porcelain on the island.

ABOVE: To create a collected feel for the kitchen, Prevost layered in different metals. The cabinets sport hardware in an oil-rubbed bronze finish, the faucet shines in polished nickel, and the statement sink is made of concrete. BELOW: In an even trade, homeowner Lisa Joyce gave her mother her fajita recipe in exchange for ideas about spice-drawer design. "I saw hers, and I knew I had to have one, too," Lisa says. "It's one of my favorite things in the kitchen."

EXPERIENCED CHEFS KNOW JUST HOW IMPORTANT GREAT TASTE AND A SENSE OF HUMOR ARE WHEN IT COMES TO CREATING NEW DISHES. California-based home cook Lisa Joyce has a heaping helping of each. "Lisa is a hoot—she really should be on television," says interior designer Melissa Prevost. "She's so quirky, and she loves to teach people how to cook. I think she needs her own show."

Unfortunately, when Prevost visited the Joyces' 1,600-square-foot bungalow for the first time, she found a galley kitchen that was not quite ready for primetime. "It was dark and didn't function well," Prevost says. "We ultimately decided to remove a large wall between the kitchen and the living room, and in doing that, we were able to achieve an open, L-shape area with space for a really nice-size island."

Once demolition was complete and the layout reconfigured, Prevost worked with Lisa to develop her personal style for the work space. "I'm not a visionary; I needed help," Lisa says. "Melissa would come over, and we'd look through magazines together. She'd send over samples of surfaces, and we'd go look at things so I could see and touch them." But even as they began layering in plenty of pretty touches—terra-cotta zellige tile, a concrete sink, and open shelving—the room's practicality remained top of mind. An industrial stainless-steel hood hovers above the bronze knobs on a six-burner range. The midnight blue-painted island is outfitted with plenty of power for an array of appliances, handy shelves for Lisa's "5 million" cookbooks, and a trash receptacle. Along the perimeter, durable, dark honed granite tops white oak cabinets.

These days, the kitchen is home to plenty of light, (smartphone) cameras, and action, as Lisa plays host to a steady stream of family and friends. "I spend most of my time here," Lisa says. "I cook constantly! My signature dish for big groups is fajitas. I have marinated steak, chicken, and vegetarian options piled high on the island, so there's a little something—and plenty of room—for everyone."

Resources begin on page 92.

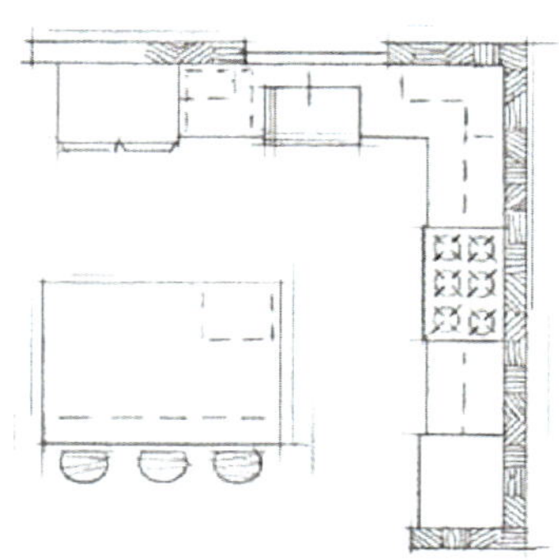

the plan

The removal of a large wall between the kitchen and the living room opened up the once-cramped space. Perimeter cabinets form an L-shape, leaving plenty of room for a spacious island to take center stage—while staying in arm's reach of the sink and range.

THIS PHOTO: Countertop clutter is kept to a minimum, thanks to the large island that provides hidden storage for appliances and kitchen equipment and display space for cookbooks and serving pieces.

DESIGNER INSIGHTS: BEAUTY MEETS FUNCTION

Follow designer Melissa Prevost's tips for making the most of a small kitchen.

• *Have a simple plan.* To create an easy-to-manage layout, Prevost asked homeowner Lisa Joyce to prioritize the appliances and tools she uses the most. "I'm never going to push aesthetic over function," Prevost says. At first, Lisa thought she needed more room. "This is actually a perfect-size space for someone who cooks every day," she says now. "Nothing is too far away."

• *Maintain balance.* Prevost knew that marble was not going to cut it in this particular kitchen due to the upkeep required. "This was only my second time using a porcelain slab, but it really brings an elevated look to the island." The advantages of the material abound—not only is it less expensive and stronger than marble and granite, it's scratch-resistant, stands up to heat, cleans up easily, and comes in lots of colors and patterns.

• *Marry style and substance.* Moroccan terra-cotta zellige tile shows up in the coolest Instagram design accounts for a reason: The delightful y imperfect-shape pieces make for a luminescent backsplash. But the material is also hardy and easily wiped down when sauce bubbles over. "It's as durable as any other material," Prevost says.

• *Aim for sensible splurges.* Because the budget wasn't unlimited and her client prioritized function over luxe finishes, Prevost hunted for budget-friendly hardware so Lisa could go big on appliances, including a pro-style range. "We had to put in a gas line. Before that, I was cooking on a flat-top electric stove," the homeowner says. "The best part of my new kitchen is having a gas range."

TUXEDO *chic*

Metallic accents and a glossy black-and-white palette elevate this California kitchen.

The kitchen's high-contrast scheme keeps the space light and airy. The run of black cabinetry includes a pantry and a paneled refrigerator and freezer.

WRITER Zlata Kozul Naumovski
PHOTOS Edmund Barr
FIELD EDITOR Karen Reinecke

AS MARSI HAUENSTEIN AND HER HUSBAND EMBARKED ON A GUT RENOVATION OF THEIR SOUTHERN CALIFORNIA HOME, the couple was sure of one thing: The kitchen had to be black and white. Classic for a reason, the color scheme has proved complementary to seasonal decor, colorful accents, and even young children.

The mix-and-match is intentional but lenient. White base cabinets contrast dark upper cabinets; black drawers accent one side of the white island. The sophisticated dark cabinetry takes center stage on one wall, concealing storage, a refrigerator, and a freezer while drawing the eye toward the back of the room, past the overscale lantern-style pendants. Trimmed in brass, the pendants echo the finish of the linear cabinet hardware, high-arc sink faucet, pot-filler faucet, and even the mesh inserts (imported from England) that line the backs of the upper cabinets flanking the ventilation hood.

"The kitchen is glamorous," says Erin McGilvery, principal of Folio Design, referencing

DESIGNER INSIGHTS: ALWAYS IN STYLE

Designer Erin McGilvery knows a thing or two about creating a striking kitchen, but the real success of an attractive space relies on its longevity. Consider these trend-transcending characteristics for a kitchen you'll love forever.

• ***Embrace a high-contrast color palette.*** Black and white is the most popular for a reason—it's classic and timeless. The sophisticated color combination works equally well in modern and traditional settings. For a softer look, consider deep navy paired with white.

• ***Deploy metallics.*** McGilvery and her client relied on satin brass as the dominant metal in the kitchen. They used it on hardware and in unexpected places, such as the mesh lining the backs of cabinets. Used sparingly, the metallic finish pops and feels special.

• ***Include furniturelike elements.*** For a relaxed, lived-in feel, consider including a banquette or other comfortable seating options. The tufted banquette in the Hauenstein kitchen conjures images of chic cafés.

TOP LEFT: Black appliances meld seamlessly into the lower cabinets. "I decided to use a big portion of the budget on heavy-duty satin-brass handles," homeowner Marsi Hauenstein says of the hardware. TOP MIDDLE: The banquette's tufting is decorative while the vinyl upholstery easily wipes clean. TOP RIGHT: With its high arc and vintage-inspired design, the satin-brass faucet is the kitchen's crown jewel.

THIS PHOTO: Matching lightly-veined quartz tops the countertops and backsplash for a seamless look.

THIS PHOTO: A glass table and wishbone dining chairs add elegance to the kitchen. **OPPOSITE:** Young children and a dog did not dissuade Marsi from choosing stools with white leather upholstery. The sides of the oversize island are detailed with paneling so it resembles furniture.

The black-and-white palette looks festive at Christmas, pretty with pastel flowers in the spring, and can easily be warmed up in the autumn months.

—MARSI HAUENSTEIN, HOMEOWNER

the gold metallic grout and shimmering glass-tile backsplash behind the wet bar. At the island, white leather stools add an extra dose of grandeur in line with the homeowners' taste. "Marsi has a really strong design sensibility," McGilvery says.

Beyond good looks, the kitchen needed to be a space the entire Hauenstein family could enjoy. McGilvery delivered with a tufted faux-leather banquette that gives the children a comfortable perch to enjoy breakfast or work on homework outside of the primary cooking zone.

The kitchen is everything Marsi and her family hoped it would be, down to the last detail. "There isn't anything I would change," Marsi says.

Resources begin on page 92.

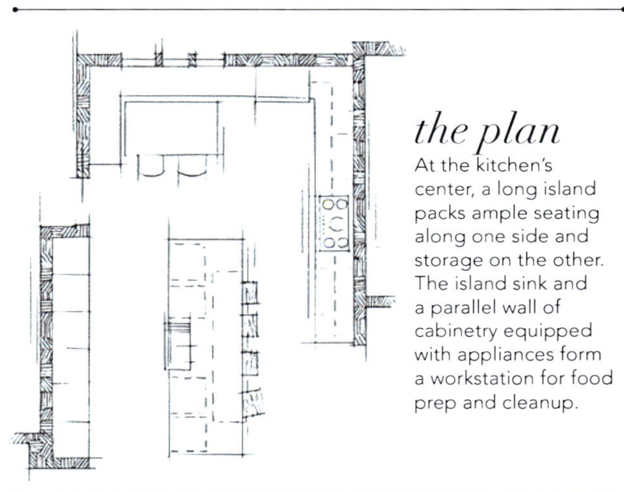

the plan

At the kitchen's center, a long island packs ample seating along one side and storage on the other. The island sink and a parallel wall of cabinetry equipped with appliances form a workstation for food prep and cleanup.

WRITER Elizabeth Sweet
PHOTOS Joyelle West
FIELD EDITOR Karin Lidbeck-Brent

LEFT: The caneback dining chairs, painted Benjamin Moore Rich Coral, add a jolt of energy to the otherwise neutral space. "The kitchen is both fresh and warm at the same time," designer Jenn Sanborn says.

Cape Cod CHARMER

A historic Colonial home is lovingly reimagined for the future.

THIS PHOTO: "I think there is an inherent beauty in a natural product, so that's always my go-to," Sanborn says of her decision to use stone instead of a manufactured countertop material.

THIS PHOTO: Walls are painted Benjamin Moore White Dove. The trim, ceiling, and perimeter cabinets are swathed in Brick House Tan. The putty shade appears on the island cabinetry's interior, too.

AFTER A RIGOROUS SEARCH, DESIGNER JENN SANBORN'S CLIENTS HAD FALLEN IN LOVE

with a Cape Cod (identical to one of architect Royal Barry Wills' designs) in the leafy coastal town of Newburyport, Massachusetts. Pedigree aside, the dark interiors of the circa-1961 home were ripe for an overhaul. The couple wished for a retirement-friendly environment suitable for aging in place and a spacious chef's kitchen.

Sanborn set to work, reconfiguring the layout and borrowing space from an existing living area to make room for a main-floor primary bedroom suite, a mudroom, and a breezeway leading to a light-filled kitchen and pantry. "We created this lovely kitchen space with a vaulted ceiling and views to the backyard," she says.

The kitchen features a double-galley layout with an adjacent dining area, a sizable multipane window, and a wood-paneled cathedral ceiling. A hardworking island with a dark finish and elegant cabinets painted Benjamin Moore Brick House Tan provide purposeful storage. Tucked away behind a space-saving pocket door is the ample new pantry. "To have that open, free-of-upper-cabinetry look, you have to put the stuff somewhere," Sanborn says.

She artfully wove in charming period details—an antique-style reproduction sink, a wall-mount faucet, turn-latch hardware, and traditional millwork—to keep new additions age-appropriate. In the center of the space, luxurious Taj Mahal quartzite countertops with a leathered finish add an air of updated luxury.

In its next phase, the historic Cape Cod and its brand-new kitchen will see morning coffee, family meals, and all the gatherings in between. "What brings me joy is that my clients can grow older in a home they just adore," Sanborn says. "That makes it all worthwhile."

Resources begin on page 92.

ABOVE: Open shelving, visible upon entry, allows for attractive jar storage. A carpenter built the shelves on-site to Sanborn's specifications. BELOW: On the island's far side, Sanborn prioritized storage over seating to make space for her clients' elegant china and crystal. Cabinets have seeded-glass fronts and contrasting painted interiors.

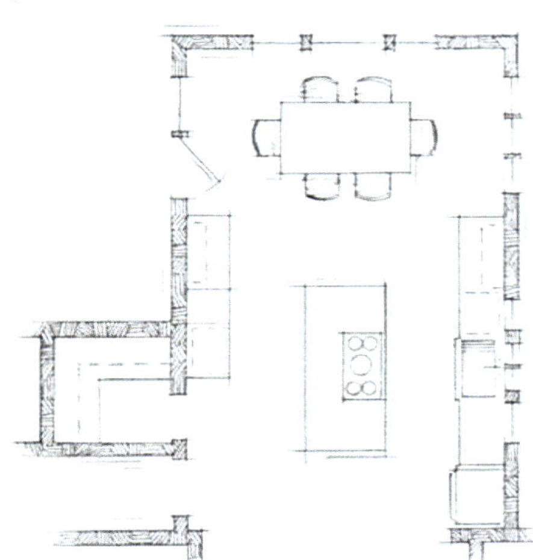

the plan

A storage-filled island with an induction cooktop anchors two hardworking walls: one with cooking appliances and one with the sink and prep area. At the back of double-galley layout, the dining room is a focal point. Walls of windows and open shelves provide a light and airy look. A nearby pantry keeps the main area clutter-free.

It's not a white kitchen. It has that rich, historical tan color, which is great because everyone has a white kitchen.

—JENN SANBORN, DESIGNER

DESIGNER INSIGHTS: PERFECT PANTRY

A character-rich kitchen deserves a pantry to match. Designer Jenn Sanborn shares her strategies for creating a space that will stand the test of time.

- ***Repeat materials.*** Sanborn used a familiar paint color and decorative paneling details to keep the pantry in conversation with the kitchen.
- ***Add custom window treatments.*** The tab-top curtains are handmade and historically appropriate. They conceal practical pullout storage from view, too, and are easy to push aside.
- ***Incorporate stone remnants.*** Leathered Tuscan Mist granite tops the pantry counter, adding permanence and charm. Plus, it's a remnant, which saved on cost.
- ***Install a pocket door.*** "Pocket doors are great if you don't want a door swing," Sanborn says, or if you just wish to add some character. For smaller spaces, they're both functional and easy on the eyes.
- ***Check the details.*** The café curtain rods, purchased on Etsy, needed to be exact, Sanborn says, as did the dimensions for the shelves set to hold appliances. To ensure everything fits as it should, carefully measure height and depth.

THIS PHOTO: A pro-style induction cooktop, steam oven, and wall oven elevate the space's cooking prowess. Shaker-style cabinet fronts conceal the refrigerator.

An easy-living waterfront kitchen is all about repurposed antiques, neutral tones, and slow-paced cooking.

RUSTIC *& Refined*

WRITER LuAnn Brandsen
PHOTOS Michael Hunter
STYLIST Jessica Brinkert Holtam

RIGHT: Zinc inset panels and height-enhancing wheels give the island a rustic, industrial vibe. FAR RIGHT: "I love to cook and wanted a kitchen with all the bells and whistles," homeowner Audrey Wylie says. "I'm happy that it's also an easy, low-maintenance kitchen to work in."

VIN
DE
SAINT EMI

THIS PHOTO: A cabinet-turned-island inspired this Texas kitchen's design—and is the main focal point. Designer Ginger Barber likes when islands don't perfectly match other cabinetry.

WHILE PERUSING A HOUSTON ANTIQUES STORE, DESIGNER GINGER BARBER AND HER CLIENT AUDREY WYLIE LOOKED at a weathered cabinet and saw different things. Audrey ran her hand across the handsome wood surface with a Belgian stone inset as she imagined the piece's previous life in a European farmhouse or bakery—and then she moved on to the next antique in sight. Barber, envisioning the classic yet unfussy kitchen Audrey had dreamed up in their meetings, had other ideas.

"She said it was a remarkable piece of furniture that would make a beautiful island," Audrey says. "And I'm thinking, *Wow! You can do that?* I always thought islands were something you built." Curiosity piqued, Audrey watched as Barber worked with a shop clerk to find a door made of similar wood that could be cut to enlarge the island's surface. When Barber suggested adding industrial wheels for height, Audrey was sold.

The salvaged island serves as a focal point in the kitchen of Audrey's Texas vacation home, where builder John Driess shaped the layout around the island's dimensions. Audrey and her husband, Forrest, wanted a family- and dog-friendly space with low-maintenance, durable surfaces and enough elbow room for Audrey to prepare brisket and gumbo with or without an audience.

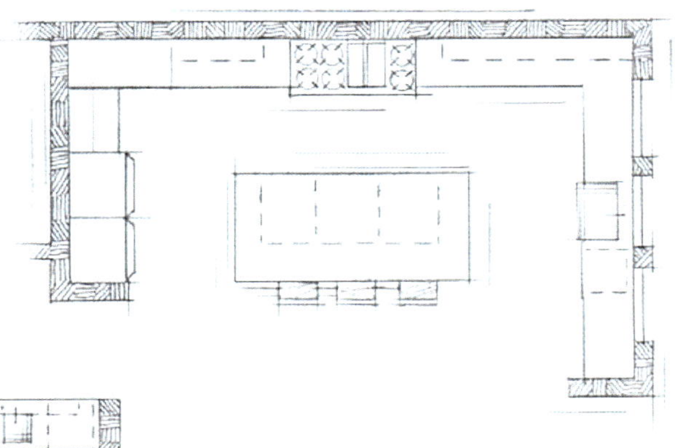

the plan

The layout is designed around the dimensions of the island, which is movable. Cooking appliances are strategically positioned to reduce steps for a busy cook. The sink sits below a window with a view of the nearby bay.

TOP: "I'm in the kitchen all the time, so I wanted to be sure the room had wonderful views overlooking the bay," Audrey says. Below the sink, chunky nickel pulls, like those you might find on a window sash, are installed horizontally to ensure they're easy to grasp. ABOVE: A vintage wine barrel lid hangs on shiplap installed edge to edge (rather than tongue-and-groove) to achieve textural lines between boards.

THIS PHOTO: Salvaged 100-year-old heart pine ceiling beams and a chunky custom-made table are a nod to Texas rusticity. Antique shutters with a gentle patina flank the bar. **OPPOSITE:** A refrigerator hides behind cabinetry.

It's not overly decorated. It's lived in.

—GINGER BARBER, DESIGNER

Barber, a minimalist designer who favors timeless whites, rich textures, and well-chosen antiques, opted for a neutral color palette to reflect the home's views of Galveston Island's bay. She added touches of Southern rusticity to ensure that simplicity reigns serene. Wood grain peeks through whitewashed shiplap walls and gray-washed oak floors. White-painted cabinets forgo panels and molding in favor of just a tiny bit of trim. Classic white-glass pendants and chalky celadon gray countertops demand little attention, while a streamlined plaster hood epitomizes the power of restraint.

"My motto is to keep it simple, and my goal is to create rooms that will look good forever," Barber says. "Not having too many things going on makes it peaceful."

Resources begin on page 92.

DESIGNER INSIGHTS: LAYERS OF INTEREST

Ginger Barber's knack for blending textured materials with neutrals is key to her timeless, uncomplicated design. Here's how she keeps white kitchens from fading away.

- ***Start at the bottom.*** Use rugs to springboard a room's design. Seagrass and wool jute lay down texture and clean easily. Vintage Oushak rugs (Turkish with strong Persian influence) unfurl a little more color and forgive spills.
- ***Keep texture key.*** Make even the most minimalist of rooms inviting with woods, woven shades, baskets, and whitewashed finishes. Elements in the same color family will read differently with varied textures, and that's what makes a space feel good.
- ***Stick with subtle surfaces.*** Countertops don't need to scream to provide impact. Barber's go-to choices include Alhambra limestone and concrete.
- ***Use the shadow effect.*** Play with various whites, noticing how they mix with the light in the room. Barber sometimes paints walls and cabinets the same color, then cuts that color by 50 percent for trim and by 75 percent for the ceiling. "It's hard to really tell what's happening," she says. "It's just interesting and easy on the eye."
- ***Think small details.*** Little changes add up. Trade brightly colored plastic utensils for wooden ones, or add a great specimen plant to an oversize basket. The visual difference can be effective.
- ***Edit carefully.*** For some, an all-white background invites an opportunity to pile on decorations. Resist! Instead, pare down your selections and let the blank canvas speak for itself.

WRITER Jenny Bradley Pfeffer
PHOTOS Julie Soefer
FIELD EDITOR Jessica Brinkert Holtam

Good as GOLD

THIS PHOTO: Designers Audrey Tehauno and Jana Erwin employed brass touches throughout the kitchen. Faucets with an unlacquered-brass finish coordinate beautifully with pendant lights and cabinet hardware in antiqued brass. **OPPOSITE:** Details abound in this spacious kitchen. Hand-painted tile on the backsplash adds a dash of charm and a pop of color to the otherwise cream-and-brown space.

A harmonious blend of elements brings old-world allure to a newly renovated Houston kitchen.

“In a large kitchen with large expanses of cabinetry, the eye needs a break.”

—AUDREY TEHAUNO, DESIGNER

ALTHOUGH BUILT JUST 15 YEARS AGO, MARGARITA AND MIKE JACOBS' HOUSTON HOME EXUDES OLD-WORLD CHARM.

Located on a tree-lined street in the city's beguiling Bellaire neighborhood, the house checked all the boxes, except one. Its small, cloistered kitchen stood in stark contrast to the rest of the large, open home. "The kitchen was closed off from the living room," Margarita says. "And although we have a large home, everyone wanted to congregate around the food, of course!"

To remedy the problem, Margarita and Mike called on Audrey Tehauno and Jana Erwin of Nest Design Group. Their solution: Commandeer space from a small, unused spare bedroom and bath to enlarge the kitchen and allow for the addition of a mudroom and pantry. "With the space we obtained from the bedroom and bath, we doubled the size of the kitchen, allowing for a space much better suited to this family," Tehauno says.

With a more spacious footprint, symmetry became a guiding force. The design team added a second window to balance the range wall that features a custom plaster hood. Two large islands punctuate the rectangular space and create

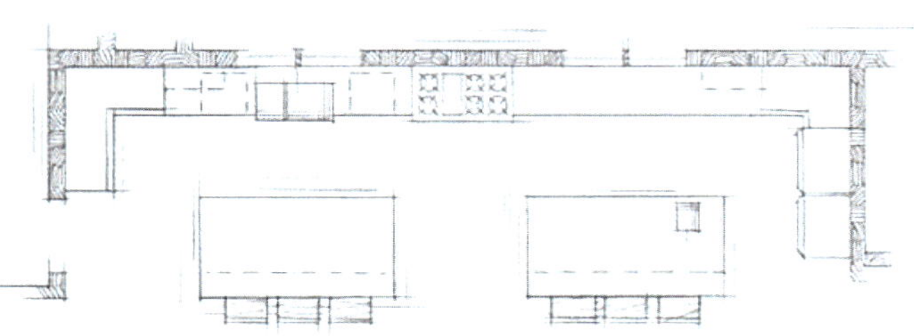

the plan

Expanding the kitchen's layout allowed designers to add dual islands as workstations and auxiliary spaces, including a mudroom and butler's pantry. Cabinetry and open shelving flank the pro-style range and keep everyday dishware easy to access.

OPPOSITE: Stations dedicated to different tasks keep the large space organized. Countertop cabinets next to the stainless-steel refrigerator house a coffee station, while a baking station and appliance garage are on the opposite side of the room. **ABOVE RIGHT:** Upper cabinets show off a creamy white finish for an airy look. **RIGHT:** Custom ironwork shelves add an industrial touch to the fanciful tile.

ABOVE: A classic-shape plaster hood was designed without ornamentation to give the eye a place to rest. For visual weight and practicality (the family has two young children and pets), lower cabinets were stained with a gray-brown finish.

separate workstations that have become the family's epicenter. "The islands are incredibly functional," Erwin says. "The kids can be doing homework or snacking at one island while Margarita preps for meals on the other. And they are ideal for entertaining."

Aesthetically, Tehauno and Erwin wanted to maintain the home's classic style, choosing timeless millwork that felt traditional but with a current flair. Cream-color upper cabinets enhance the kitchen's light, airy appeal. For contrast, visual weight, and camouflaging wear and tear, lower cabinets are stained dark brown with a hint of gray.

A mix of metal finishes—oil-rubbed-bronze hardware, unlacquered-brass fixtures, ironwork shelves, and antiqued-brass pendants over the islands—creates a balance between masculine and feminine, formal and casual. The pièce de résistance, however, is the custom, hand-painted tile. It plays equally well with the industrial nature of the open ironwork shelving and the simplicity of the plaster hood—both of which were designed to complement the tile's intricate pattern. "We wanted the eye to go to the backsplash first," Erwin says. "The other elements, from the simple window shades to the open shelving, were all chosen to allow the tile to be the showstopper."

Resources begin on page 92.

THIS PHOTO: The pantry offers additional storage space for the homeowner's collection of dishes. Details and finishes mirror those used in the kitchen.

DESIGNER INSIGHTS: NAVIGATING A LARGE FOOTPRINT

Designers Audrey Tehauno and Jana Erwin made decisions with the kitchen's new ample square footage in mind.

- ***Let major appliances stand out against cabinet panels.*** "In a large kitchen with large expanses of cabinetry, the eye needs a break," Erwin says. "We kept the stainless fronts for balance."
- ***Implement dual islands.*** Two islands prevent the kitchen from feeling too empty while offering additional counter space, storage, and kitchen function. One island can be reserved for meal prep while the other can be a place to gather.
- ***Think symmetrically***. The designers expanded the kitchen while ensuring the space is visually balanced: three barstools for each island, two pendants above, and matching cabinetry on either side of the range.

WRITER Sally Finder Weepie
PHOTOS Michael Kaskel

smooth BLEND

A suburban Chicago kitchen melds elements from multiple eras into a cooking and gathering space for the ages.

OPPOSITE: Black cabinetry and handmade tile dial up the drama in the bar area of the butler's pantry. **THIS PHOTO:** Brass interiors on pendant lights over the island mesh with unlacquered brass on hardware and the traditional-style faucet.

When designer Rebekah Zaveloff couldn't find a marble slab long enough for the island she envisioned, she took inspiration from a vintage French cabinet and trimmed the marble with wood.

FORGET BURNT ORANGE, LAVA LAMPS, AND DISCO.

Designer Rebekah Zaveloff and her friend Lorie FitzGibbon love the 1970s, but when they wanted to bring a touch of their childhood to Lorie's new Chicago-area kitchen, they plucked only elements that have evolved into classics—well-traveled boho, geometric pattern, sultry brass, textural rattan and cane—to be part of their timeless blend.

"Lorie and I grew up together in Ohio," says Zaveloff, cofounder and principal designer at KitchenLab Interiors. "We were both heavily influenced by the style of the late '70s and early '80s—boho/hippie meets disco and glam."

So when Lorie and husband John started work on a new home, she knew where to find her muse. "I love the character that comes with old houses, and I wanted to give that aesthetic to Lorie in a home with casual elegance," Zaveloff says. The key, the friends agreed, was bringing elements from past eras into the new interiors.

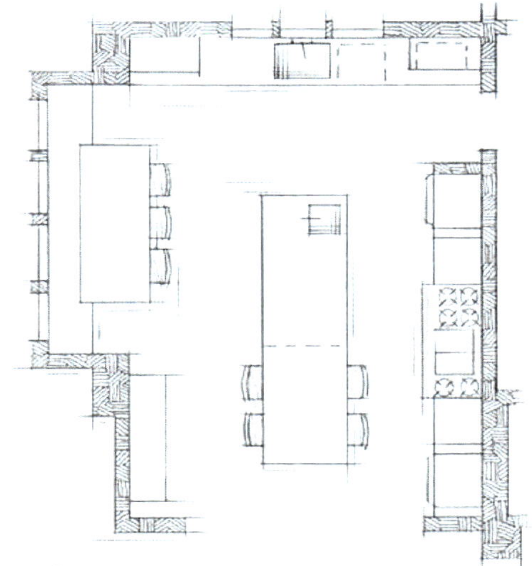

the plan

A long island separates functions, with the cooking zone on one side and a breakfast nook and additional storage on the other. Along the back wall of cabinetry and paneled appliances, the kitchen's main sink has a prime spot below the window.

That viewpoint is evident in Lorie's kitchen, where fads are forbidden and the magic is in the mix. White-painted upper cabinets serve as a classic foil to the warm, organic vibe of riftsawn white oak. At the same time, traditional crown moldings play off the farmhouse simplicity of a shiplap-covered range hood. A newly built wood-and-glass hutch reflects the craftsmanship of an earlier era, giving it the venerable feel of a family heirloom. An inset marble top brings the element of surprise to a classic Mission-style table that doubles as the kitchen island. White quartzite countertops recede, allowing the spotlight to fall on two distinctly different backsplashes: marblelike porcelain in a modern slab format behind the range, and terra-cotta tile with a geometric bronze inlay behind the sink. Contemporary black accents marry with ageless unlacquered brass. "There is no one style, no one era," Zaveloff says. "It's about how materials interact."

A pro-style double range, two sinks, a built-in microwave, and undercounter refrigerator drawers that supplement the panel-cloaked main fridge meet all the needs of a busy mom getting dinner on the table every night.

"I love this house," Lorie says. "There's so much of me—and Rebekah—in here. It feels good, like our childhood. And that's a really happy feeling."

Resources begin on page 92.

ABOVE: A panel that looks like a door to a pantry closet stylishly hides the refrigerator/freezer. FAR LEFT: A sleek microwave oven is positioned into the cabinetry in the back of the kitchen, forming a workstation that is out of the way. LEFT: On the other side of the back wall, a double-drawer refrigerator is concealed by cabinetry panels. The under-the-counter appliance keeps beverages cool and within reach.

DESIGNER INSIGHTS: MIXING ERAS

Want a new kitchen to have the look—and character—of a space that has evolved over time? Bring in a blend of styles and eras.

• ***Count on the classics.*** Designer Rebekah Zaveloff eschews one-hit wonders from any era. Pick elements with staying power to build a blend that's collected, not chaotic. Shaker cabinets? Marble and wood? They're in style yesterday, today, and always.

• ***Repeat yourself.*** Don't mix things up too much. Pair different styles of cabinets or different species of wood as long as nothing feels random. Repeat wood or white-painted elements, for example, so there's eye-pleasing continuity across styles.

• ***Follow your heart.*** Create a signature moment or two with elements you love, like Lorie FitzGibbon's geometric-pattern backsplash and caneback, tubular-steel barstools (a '70s favorite descended from Marcel Breuer's classic 1928 Cesca design.

ABOVE: The kitchen connects to a comfortable breakfast area where the entire family can share a meal—and time—together. A new hutch built to look like an old piece contrasts the island's white oak trim.

> There is no one style, no one era. It's about how materials interact.
>
> —REBEKAH ZAVELOFF, DESIGNER

LEFT: A window over an apron-front sink is a timeless move. An arch shape flanked by sculptural lamps makes it riveting. **THIS PHOTO:** Designer Julie Zich's kitchen is a luxe mix of gold and blue accents.

family TIES

For her own kitchen, a designer channeled her childhood memories to create a space that welcomes all.

WRITER Kathryn O'Shea-Evans
PHOTOS Werner Straube
FIELD EDITOR Hilary Rose

THIS PHOTO: Glamorous pendants illuminate the island. "They have layers upon layers of glass, which creates this beautiful sparkle," Julie says.

SUBDUED IS NOT DESIGNER JULIE ZICH'S STYLE, ESPECIALLY WHEN IT COMES TO HER FAMILY'S NEWLY BUILT GEORGIAN AND GREEK REVIVAL-STYLE HOME IN WESTERN SPRINGS, ILLINOIS.

"The goal was to make it look different than what I've seen everywhere else," she says. "I wanted it to have a real warmth—the warmth of the past, the warmth of my childhood."

Much of the inspiration for the space came from Julie's ancestry. "I didn't realize this until we were doing the home, but so much of the way that I was designing was based on my own childhood," she says. "We're Italian. And my grandfather used to make homemade pasta and homemade pasta sauce, and my sisters and cousins and I would all sit around him, dipping our bread in." So it's no surprise that one of Julie's top priorities was to have an island where her entire brood and their friends could gather. "That island was probably the most important thing to me in the kitchen," she says. When the project's architect Brad Lewis suggested inserting two islands—one for prep and one for gathering—Julie stood firm. "I needed it all together,"

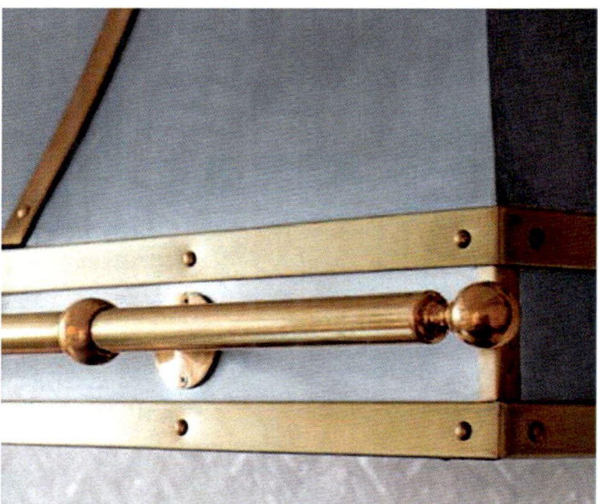

CLOCKWISE FROM TOP LEFT: There's no such thing as too much storage in a cookspace—one reason why Julie tucked shelves into the walls of her island's built-in seating banquette. Julie designed the tall, brass-strapped range hood herself and had Custom Copper Hoods, Inc. build it. The white-on-white kitchen trend didn't hold enough interest for Julie, so for the hutch-like cabinetry flanking the sink she opted for a deep walnut wood with custom brass pulls. "The brass warms it all up," she says.

THIS PHOTO: A long lighting fixture that echoes the length of the table can cast an entire dinner party in a soft, romantic glow. **OPPOSITE:** Powder blue cabinetry and curvaceous trim on the glass doors make even the butler's pantry memorable.

I wanted it to have a real warmth—the warmth of the past, the warmth of my childhood.

—JULIE ZICH, HOMEOWNER AND DESIGNER

she says, noting that sometimes there can be 10 kids at the house at one time. "That was really important to me."

The designer's other must? "I wanted the room to look fabulous," she says. To that end, the team installed an arch window over the sink, glamorous rich walnut cabinetry with gleaming brass pulls, and—the ultimate eye candy—Tiffany Blue upholstery in kitchen-friendly wipeable vinyl. "It's just such a cheerful, beautiful color!" Julie says. "I wanted a luxe vibe, for it to feel warm and welcoming, but rich." Mission accomplished.

Resources begin on page 92.

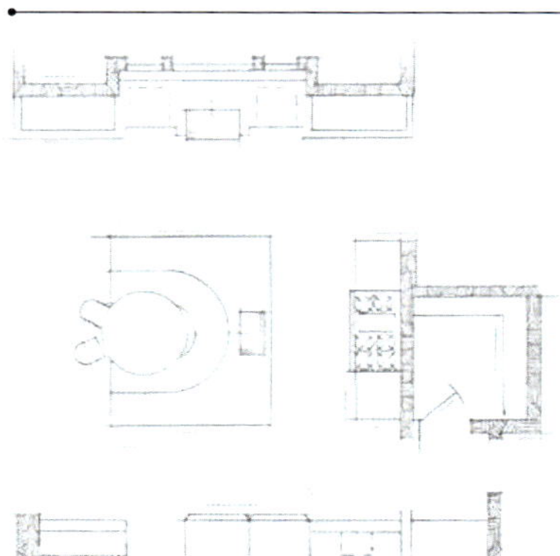

the plan

Natural light pours in from a large arch window above the main sink. At the kitchen's center, a C-shape island tucks banquette seating in one side and an additional sink on the other.

DESIGNER INSIGHTS: MORE THAN MEETS THE EYE

An unfussy, sophisticated kitchen design, according to designer Julie Zich, calls for concealed appliances and hidden storage. "This allows all who enter to focus on the detail and real beauty of the room," she says. These are her favorites.

- ***An integrated dishwasher.*** "This drawer in the island blends right in and matches the rest of the kitchen, giving the space an almost peaceful feel. Plus, it's positioned next to the island sink, so that all cookware and bakeware go directly into the dishwasher."

- ***Push-to-open cabinetry.*** "This invisible cabinetry looks like simple paneling added to finish off the island fronts, and the fact that it has no hardware helps keep my secret! I love how we maximized the space, leaving no open area wasted."

- ***A warming drawer.*** "This one may take the cake! Often, one member of the family is unable to join the rest of us for dinner. The warming drawer hidden behind pocket doors allows me to wrap up the dinner and keep it warm."

LIGHT *Touch*

WRITER Paula M. Bodah
PHOTOS Jason Donnelly
STYLIST Lisa Evidon
FIELD EDITOR Andrea Nordstrom Caughey

Stripping away dark and dated finishes reveals a Minnesota kitchen's true potential.

THIS PHOTO: The original square island was replaced with a slimmer version topped with a 2½-inch-thick slab of quartz. **OPPOSITE:** The light fixtures hung in the old kitchen, too. "It's always nice when you can give something a bit of new life," designer Elizabeth Darth says.

FAR LEFT: The kitchen faucet's finish has a warm, rosy glow. LEFT: Seasonal flowers add a dash of color to the otherwise muted kitchen. OPPOSITE: The La Cornue range, with its distinctive stainless-steel and brass trim, is a statement piece. The decorative corbels on the hood are similar to those used on the island.

OFTEN IN A DESIGN PROJECT, IT'S IMPORTANT TO FIRST NOTE WHAT IS WORKING BEFORE TAKING A SLEDGEHAMMER TO IT ALL. This Wayzata, Minnesota, kitchen—the heart and hub of the home for a family of four—had its redeeming qualities: generous dimensions, ample cabinetry, and a beloved second oven. "The bones were good," says designer Elizabeth Darth of Martha O'Hara Interiors. But the surfaces were gloomy and outmoded: the knotty alder cabinetry, the walnut floors, the deep golden-brown color of the flecked granite countertops, and the travertine backsplash tiles.

Darth and builder Dorian Thompson undertook a bottom-to-top makeover, starting with the dark floors. After much deliberation, the design pros settled on a bleaching process that gave the wood its current warm glow. "It still has a lot of color," Thompson says, "but lightening it took it from dated to fresh."

Overhead, they filled in the recess in the ceiling above the island. "Sometimes these architectural details don't really work," Darth says. And in between, they reworked everything, including replacing all the brown cabinetry with gleaming, light-reflecting white. "We had a lot of discussions about color, about possibly doing an accent color at the island, before we decided to do all white," Darth says. "It's classic and timeless."

DESIGNER INSIGHTS: WARM NOTES

Designer Elizabeth Darth says a kitchen should feel inviting and clean, not cold and sterile. Here's her winning combination.

- ***Bring in the brass.*** "Warm brass tones are a great accent in hardware, plumbing, and lighting, and provide a nice contrast with white," she says. Consider unlacquered or hand-brushed brass, which develops a soft patina over time.
- ***Prioritize movement.*** To add a sense of movement, depth, and texture, for the countertops Darth suggests a material like the delicately veined quartz she selected for this kitchen rather than pure white. For a more modern look, she used the same quartz for both the countertops and backsplash.
- ***Add subtle color.*** Nuanced shades that suggest nature, like the soft coral in the runner and the earthy hue of the woven counter stools, offers an extra layer of interest without compromising the room's serenity.

THIS PHOTO: The custom wet bar includes a beverage fridge. The small cabinet next to the sink holds a well-used electric hot cocoa mixer. **OPPOSITE LEFT:** The homeowner handpicked the cast-iron apron-front sink. The existing window was enlarged to give the family a better view of the backyard. **OPPOSITE RIGHT:** Woven rattan stools add texture and color. Darth chose a delicately veined quartz for the countertops and backsplash walls. "It creates a bit of movement and interest," she says. At the kitchen sink, the quartz rises to the ceiling, framing the window for a seamless, unified look.

We had a lot of discussions about color before deciding to go with all white. It's classic and timeless.

—ELIZABETH DARTH, INTERIOR DESIGNER

The clunky square island was swapped out for one longer, narrower, and turned so the stools face the window instead of the stove. The new island's decorative feet and corbels give it a furniturelike look, Darth says. The new cabinets stretch to meet wide molding at the ceiling, an expanse that might have felt imposing if not for the honey-bronze cabinet hardware Darth used for a warm touch. The stately La Cornue range, the homeowners' pride and joy, sports brushed-brass and stainless-steel trim and knobs, furthering the warm feel. The range hood's decorative corbels echo those on the island.

One or two of the kitchen's original elements survived the transition. To the homeowners' delight, the second oven and its companion microwave fit nicely into their new surroundings, a small reminder of just how far this kitchen has come.

Resources begin on page 92.

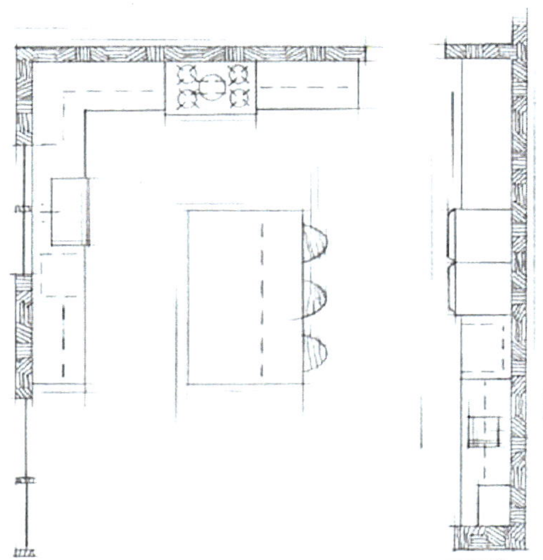

the plan

A rectangular island, with three barstools facing the window, separates the kitchen's workstation from a cleanup area. Dual ovens, a refrigerator, and a wet bar allow the homeowners to grab and prepare food in one spot.

Surface Appeal

With all the tile and stone they could want at their fingertips, two designers dream up a subtly elegant bath.

WRITER Samantha Stevenson
PHOTOS Edmund Barr
STYLIST Char Hatch Langos

For John and Eileen Huarte, founders and owners of Arizona Tile, their primary bath was an opportunity to showcase some of their favorite products. "We knew we wanted to highlight our slabs," Eileen says of the Calacatta marble blanketing the vanities, tub casing, and shower and bathroom walls.

DESIGNER INSIGHTS: SMALL-SPACE HACKS

A bath doesn't have to be grand in size to feel spacious. Here's how interior designers Caren Rideau and Michele Trout made the most of this bath's square footage.

• ***Keep the room open.*** Dual vanities, the tub, and the shower sit flush against opposing walls, making a U configuration. The layout makes the bath appear spacious but not empty. "It's easy to move around in but not over-the-top big," Rideau says. "It's still inviting."

• ***Create built-in storage.*** Rideau took a foot from the water closet to create a recessed linen closet. "When a closet is not protruding into the bath, you get a more spacious look," she says.

• ***Design around windows.*** "We had a view straight out to the Pacific Ocean," Trout says. "The room is flooded with sunlight."

• ***Employ metallic finishes.*** The material's reflectivity can maximize the natural light and make a space feel airy.

CLOCKWISE FROM TOP: In the roomy shower, the design team implemented grab bars to accommodate aging in place. Inset shelving creates a high-end look while keeping the shower clutter-free. A sleek faucet in a nickel finish acts in ensemble with the bath's other soft-but-luxe features. "I like using small patterns on bathroom floors," designer Caren Rideau says of the decorative marble. "The more grouted it is, the less slippery it is." A bouquet of pink peonies stands out against the bath's gentle palette but echoes the vibrant nature just past the window. The twin mirrored medicine cabinets are made from nickel, complementing the finish of the light fixtures, faucets, towel holders, and pulls.

ABOVE: Dual vanities give the room a sense of symmetry. The two pieces, dressed in the same marble as the rest of the bath, blend into the surrounding stone. White cabinetry and clean-line hardware and sconces achieve a low-key glamorous look. "The homeowners are not over-the-top, so we didn't want to make the bath over-the-top," Rideau says. "The bath is understated for how luxurious it is."

HOW DOES A DESIGNER SHOW RESTRAINT WHEN AN ENTIRE PORTFOLIO OF RESOURCES IS WITHIN REACH? When the owners of Arizona Tile, John and Eileen Huarte, enlisted designers Caren Rideau of Kitchen Design Group and Michele Trout of Bonesteel Trout Hall to transform rooms of their newly built home, the primary bath became an opportunity to display the couple's products. The designers relished the endless possibilities but were wary of going too far. They clung to the ethos that less is more.

The Huartes wanted their ocean-view bath to feel spacious, accommodate twin vanities, and have grand but relaxed features. "You could really dress the bath up," Rideau says, "but the challenge was maintaining the elegance and stature it deserves."

Simple sophistication started with Calacatta marble, which appears on the vanity countertops, on the tub surround, and inside the walk-in shower. On the marble floor, a subtle diamond pattern adds visual interest. For contrast, the design team painted the wood panels cladding the tub a soft blue.

In keeping with the bath's muted palette, Rideau and Trout chose classic polished-nickel fixtures and simple recessed medicine cabinets above the vanities. Tailored sconces with white linen shades flank the medicine cabinets. Overhead, an oversize pendant grabs attention. "The large sphere sets the tone for the whole space when you walk in," Rideau says. It's unfussy but chic—which is just what the Huartes ordered.

Resources begin on page 92.

> "The space was not exceptionally large, but I wanted a bathroom that would feel as spacious as possible."
>
> —EILEEN HUARTE, HOMEOWNER

the plan

The design team created an airy-feeling retreat complete with dual vanities, a walk-in shower, a water closet, and a tub positioned below a pair of windows to take advantage of ocean views. Storage features, including a recessed linen closet, keep the bath uncluttered.

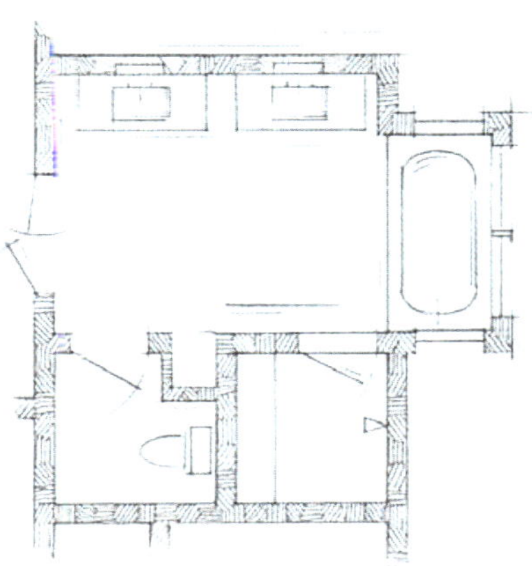

WRITER Mara Boo
PHOTOS Edmund Barr
FIELD EDITOR Karen Reinecke

Naturally MODERN

The warmth of farmhouse style dips to California cool in this contemporary bath.

White oak engineered hardwood floors unite the large space. "Tile would have been a traditional choice for flooring," interior designer Leigh Lincoln says, "but with a lot of other stone surfaces at play, we opted for a natural and organic material instead."

> Mixing metals adds depth and texture and makes the room feel more custom. The key is to keep the mix simplified.
>
> —LEIGH LINCOLN, INTERIOR DESIGNER

TOP: "The footless base and rimless lip are contemporary, while the shape is classic and substantial," Lincoln says of the bath's tub. "The two-tone effect gives the tub a weighty appearance that anchors the space, connects the two vanities through a common color palette, and adds an element of the unexpected." ABOVE LEFT: "We love to mix metals in bathrooms," Lincoln says. She advises choosing a common metal and finish for all plumbing fixtures, and a neutral complement for other hardware. ABOVE MIDDLE: Glazed ceramic subway tiles line shower walls; the floor is Calacatta Gold marble. ABOVE RIGHT: A built-in cabinet custom-crafted of riftsawn white oak offers both storage and display space. Vintage decorative accents contribute charm and convey the contemporary farmhouse look Lincoln aimed for.

WHEN YOU LIVE IN CALIFORNIA AND ARE ACCUSTOMED TO BEACHY EASE but also admire the homespun nature of modern farmhouses, you call interior designer Leigh Lincoln to converge the two. At least, that's what the owners of this newly gutted and remodeled bathroom did. "It's a fairly white bathroom," says Lincoln, cofounder of Pure Salt Interiors, who conjured the space to give the busy parents of four active kids a serene, spa-like haven. "What sets it apart are all the special touches that warm it up and make it feel welcoming and full of character, rather than cold and stark."

To wit, coastal stalwarts such as light-color wood floors, clean white cabinetry, and natural accessories mingle easily with riftsawn oak millwork, hand-painted terra-cotta tile, and matte black hardware to root an updated farmhouse aesthetic. It's a deft mix of high and low, primitive and engineered, rustic and refined—all united by Lincoln's keen sense of decorative restraint, and her belief in the power of juxtaposition.

Take the wood floors, for example, which are a warming, textural counterpoint to the luxe marble grounding the shower. The nook-residing bathtub itself is a study in contrasts thanks to its timeless white interior and edgy black exterior. Or consider the mélange of metals, featuring polished-nickel plumbing fixtures, matte black cabinet hardware, and brass-canopied pendant lighting. "Mixing metals adds depth and texture and makes the room feel more custom," Lincoln says. "The key is to keep the mix simplified."

Simple, in fact, is the room's watchword: without extraneous and unnecessary details and infused with natural elements of the earth and sea. Relaxed, indeed.

Resources begin on page 92.

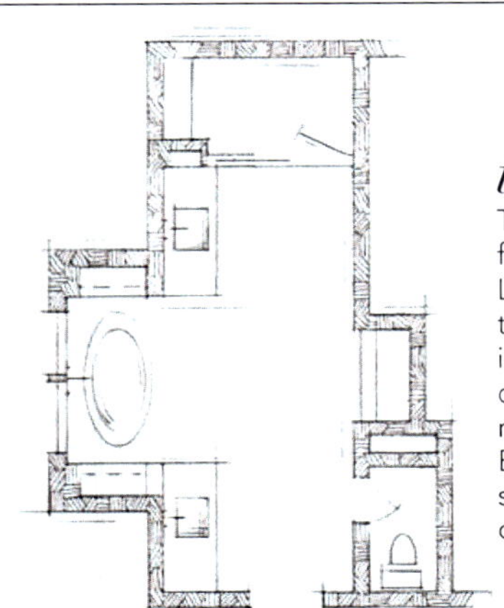

the plan

The bathroom's large footprint allowed designer Leigh Lincoln to give the tub its own space, cozied into an architectural nook centered between a matching pair of vanities. Built-in cabinetry and shelving keep the bath organized.

DESIGNER INSIGHTS: TILE WITH PERSONALITY

Patterned tile adds character in unexpected ways. For a display that breaks up a space without complete disruption, designer Leigh Lincoln follows these rules.

- ***Create a focal point.*** Define an accent wall with tile for instant impact. You could do the same with water-resistant wallcovering, but tile is an even more moisture-hardy choice. Select tile with a subtle satin sheen so splashes from the sink will easily wipe away without leaving a trace.

- ***Choose grout wisely.*** Grout color is hugely important. Had Lincoln opted for a contrasting grout color rather than one that matches the tile's off-white background, the grout would have risked overpowering both the tile itself and the bathroom as a whole, destroying her goal of a calming aesthetic. Ask your tile setter to do a grout test by tipping a handful of each of your unmixed color options between a few tiles to compare results.

- ***Plan for the expense.*** Hand-painted custom tiles can be pricey. To balance costs and ensure the statement backsplash she wanted fit within her budget, Lincoln specified wallet-friendly glazed ceramic subway tile in the shower. "It achieved the overall look we were going for but at a more affordable price," she says. "It goes to show you can pair splurge and save materials to create a custom look without any loss of design or character."

In a nod to Hollywood Regency, a Texas bath is designed with ample glass and opulent details.

HOLLYWOOD *heyday*

WRITER Zlata Kozul Naumovski
PHOTOS Julie Soefer
FIELD EDITOR Jessica Brinkert Holtam

OPPOSITE: A freestanding tub is positioned to take advantage of the above window's natural light. The nearby vanity and swivel chair give the homeowner a place to get ready. THIS PHOTO: Interior designers Nancy Bulhon and Julia B. Collins used rich woods (the vanities and cabinetry) and gold accents (the hardware, mirror, and faucet) to create a sophisticated bath reminiscent of Hollywood's Golden Age.

THIS PHOTO: Candelabra sconces with textured glass and gold accents add to the bath's vintage flair. **BELOW:** Geometric pulls in a polished-brass finish pop against the dark wood vanity.

THOUGH ROOTED IN AUSTIN, TEXAS, JULIE AND BEN CRENSHAW HAVE A LOVE FOR CALIFORNIA ARCHITECTURE.

The couple knew they wanted to inject a bit of Hollywood glamour in the South when they decided to build a new home in the Tarrytown neighborhood. Architect Ryan Street and interior designers Nancy Bulhon and Julia B. Collins looked to the influence of renowned architect Paul R. Williams, who artfully blended Hollywood Regency and Georgian styles in the 1930s, in helping the Crenshaws build their new nest.

The first certified African-American architect west of the Mississippi, Williams designed homes mostly in Southern California for celebrity clients such as Frank Sinatra, Lucille Ball, and Desi Arnaz. "His work especially resonated with Julie, who grew up in Los Angeles, surrounded by this architecture," Bulhon says. Julie introduced it to her husband, a professional golfer and two-time Masters Tournament champ, who fell in love with the style, too. "Hollywood Regency is their vibe."

For the primary bathroom, ample amounts of glass and opulent details like unlacquered brass figure prominently. One entire wall overlooks greenery from their home's hillside location while a window above the sculptural tub offers views of a lake. "It was a design challenge working in a mirror and light fixtures around all the windows," Bulhon says. She cleverly placed a gleaming custom geometric mirror, which mimics the shape of the brass hardware found on the walnut vanity and storage cabinet, on the trim in between windows. Motorized shades tuck into the ceiling to minimize visual clutter.

Marble countertops in Calacatta Borghini pick up the warm tones of the brass accents and contrast with the cool tones of the white marble flooring. That same white marble repeats in the frameless glass shower, which boasts both a rain showerhead and wall-mount fixtures for a truly luxurious experience. As a finishing touch, Bulhon dressed up one wall with a panel of polished mosaic marble tiles that effortlessly bridge the gap between past and present. Paul R. Williams would surely approve.

Resources begin on page 92.

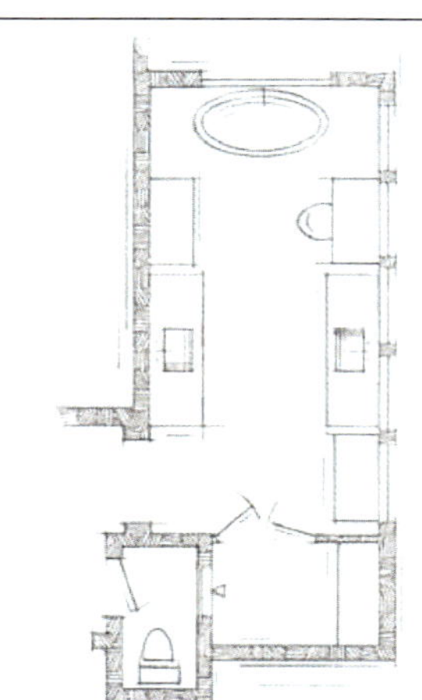

the plan

Custom vanities sit parallel, flush against the wall and flanked by an armoire on one side and a vanity on the other. A freestanding tub sits at one end; the water closet and a walk-in shower are at the other.

DESIGNER INSIGHTS: HOLLYWOOD REGENCY

The style is eclectic and glamorous with contrasting colors and textures. Here's how to capture the look.

• ***Choose the right finishes.*** Crystal sconces and brass cabinet hardware and plumbing fixtures signify opulence and offer reflective surfaces to bounce light around. The dark stain on the cabinets contrasts with the white marble and pale walls.

• ***Design various storage options.*** Rather than running same-height cabinetry, add interest with storage units of varied sizes and heights. Here, a low vanity table and tall storage unit topped with crown molding mimic the look of freestanding furniture.

• ***Accessorize appropriately.*** A vanity stool in white leather and acrylic plastic and a custom geometric brass mirror hark back to the 1930s. Underfoot, a vintage Oushak rug adds color and a sense of history.

LEFT: This bath's grandeur is in its details: The countertops are dressed in Calacatta Borghini marble, and the U-spout faucet and cross knobs have brass patina.

WRITER Sarah Egge
PHOTOS Julie Soefer
FIELD EDITOR Jessica Brinkert Holtam

Simple SPLENDOR

A personal sanctuary with top-notch amenities is the just-right antidote to one mom's full schedule.

THIS PHOTO: By choosing rectangular tiles in two sizes, chair rail trim pieces, and small hexagonal tiles for the floor, designer Alex Elam introduced geometric variety and interest in the large, tiled shower. A separate articulating showerhead is handy for the built-in bench.

THIS PHOTO: A vintage stool that Elam found at an antiques booth in Round Top, Texas, echoes the timeworn patina of the early-19th-century French cabinet.

THIS PHOTO: Large limestone tiles lead the eye to the sink, which is graced by a 1930s French mirror. A tall corner cabinet provides plenty of storage. Simple Shaker-style cabinets have a clean, tidy profile. Remnants from the Pasha marble countertops were cut to create the casing around the glass shower enclosure. "Using those big pieces means the casing is seamless and clean-looking," Elam says.

DESIGNER INSIGHTS: TO THE TOUCH

A bath should have visual and tactile interest. Designer Alex Elam brings in texture at every opportunity.

• ***Skip slick finishes*** in favor of matte, honed, tumbled, or patinaed. "The antique limestone floor tiles have pits and cracks in them, which brings in so much interest," Elam says. "The countertops are leathered. The shower tile has an antiqued hand to it, which really gives it some depth."

• ***Avoid large, flat planes.*** For example, uninterrupted wall expanses can read as dull. Tile floors with grout lines create pattern underfoot, and niches carved into the walls around the bathtub keep that area from being a boring box. Elam added a chair rail of molding-profile tile in the shower.

• ***Mix in materials*** that have "crunch," as Elam calls it. "Something with patina, that's a little crusty and peely, really warms up a space," she says. "The antique cabinet brings in the crunch." Other textural enhancement comes from small add-ins: A vintage oil painting has raised brushstrokes, crystal eau de toilette bottles are faceted, and antique books have linen or leather bindings and papery edges.

"THIS TRULY IS A LUXURIOUS BATH," INTERIOR DESIGNER ALEX ELAM says of the space she created for a busy Houston mom. "She wanted her own bathroom that would feel light and fresh and filled with natural light."

Tucked between a water closet and the primary bedroom, the space is long and narrow with a window at one end. To help daylight reach throughout the room—and to fulfill the homeowner's wish for a bright and airy feeling—Elam pulled from a subtle palette of white, ivory, pale gray, and barely tan in choosing finishes that would have a high-end look and feel. Heated limestone tiles imported from France line the floors. "The warm floors and the chrome towel warmer we found in England were real splurges," Elam says.

Turkish marble countertops pair with elegant marble tiles in the walk-in shower. Elam selected the tiles for their interesting surface texture; they don't feel slick and cold. The walls benefit from a hand-applied plaster finish that has subtle undulation and a suedelike look.

A custom vanity and makeup table conceal ample storage and offer additional get-ready space. Next to the freestanding tub, an antique cabinet holds towels and other sundries. "I must have looked at 20 different cabinets, but none were quite right," Elam says. "I found this one very close to the end of construction." The 19th-century French piece isn't the only antique delivering charm and patina to the space: An Art Deco-style mirror found in the South of France crowns the sink and reflects the view and light from the window. "I love how the 1930s mirror contrasts with the polished-nickel-and-acrylic sconces on either side for that old-and-new blend," Elam says.

After a long and busy day with her kids, the homeowner is thankful to have this quiet spot to unwind. And Elam is grateful to have played her part in it. "It doesn't get much better than this," she says.

Resources begin on page 92.

ABOVE: Vintage brass trays for jewelry or eau de toilette bottles tie into brass details used elsewhere in the house. "I always mix metals," Elam says. "And I work in brass intentionally because I think it brings warmth to all the other cool metals like nickel."

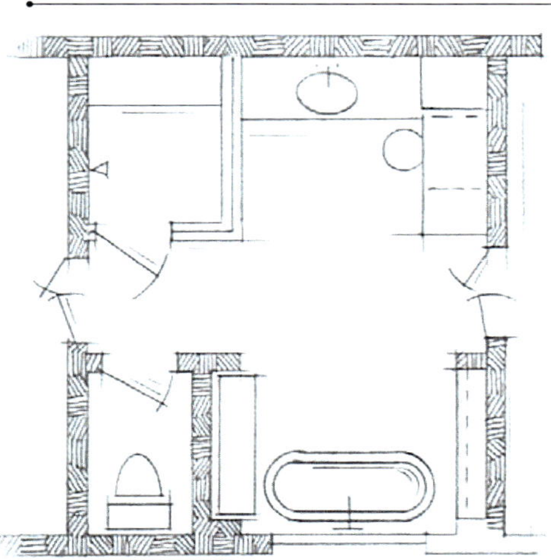

the plan

An L-shape vanity tucks a sink, drawers, and a spot to get ready into a corner of this well-organized bath. An antique French cabinet offers additional storage and flanks a freestanding tub. A walk-in shower sits parallel to the water closet.

ABOVE: A display of vintage accessories infuses the bathroom with character. Elam had this niche mirrored to reflect room-brightening light and make the tub area seem larger. Glass canisters hold bath salts, and books and fresh flowers are softening touches for all the gleaming glass surfaces. **LEFT:** This bath faucet matches the showerheads and sink faucet and is part of a classically inspired suite of polished-nickel-and-porcelain fixtures from French plumbing company Horus.

RESOURCES

For further information about products or professionals featured in *Beautiful Kitchens & Baths*™ magazine, please contact these sources. Addresses and phone numbers have been verified, but we cannot guarantee availability of items or services.

ON THE COVER

Architecture and design: Jenn Sanborn, ASID, Sacris Design, Amesbury, Massachusetts; Instagram @sacrisdesign; *sacrisdesign.com*.

IDEA GALLERY: BEHIND THE SCENES

Pages 10–15

Design: Caren Rideau, Kitchen Design Group, 15415 Sunset Blvd., Suite 106, Palisades, CA 90272; 310/454-6447; caren@kitchendesigngroup.com; Instagram @thekitchendesigngroup; *kitchendesigngroup.com*.

READY FOR A CLOSE-UP

Pages 30–33

Design: Melissa Prevost, M. Prevost Design, 270 N. El Camino Real #F462, Encinitas, CA 92024; 323/819-5367; melissa@mprevostdesign.com; Instagram @mprevostdesign; *mprevostdesign.com*.

Builder: Pete Oriol Remodeling, 4867 Mansfield St., San Diego, CA 92116; peteoriol@sbcglobal.net; 619/279-3395. **Cabinetry** custom—San Diego Custom Cabinetry; *sdcustomcabinets.com*. **Perimeter countertop** Honed Granite—Arizona Tile; *arizonatile.com*. **Island countertop** Ascale by Tau Vagli in Gold—Stone Systems; *stonesystems.us*. **Backsplash tile** Weathered White—Cle Tile; *cletile.com*. **Dishwasher, range, refrigerator, freezer**—GE Café, *cafeappliances.com*. **Range hood**—Zephyr; *zephyronline.com*. **Sink**—Native Trails; *nativetrailshome.com*. **Faucet** Brizo—Ferguson Plumbing; *ferguson .com*. **Barstools**—Boraam Industries; *boraamindustries.com*. **Runner**—Target Stores; *target.com*. **Pendants over island**—Restoration Hardware; *rh.com*. **Sconces over floating shelves**—Olde Brick Lighting; *oldebricklighting.com*. **Flooring** The Mission Collection in Cortona—Rayo Flooring; *rayowholesale.com*. **Windows** Andersen 100—Dixieline; *dixieline.com*.

TUXEDO CHIC

Pages 34–39

Design: Erin McGilvery, Folio, 1555 Camino Del Mar, Suite 105, Del Mar, CA 92014; 858/350-5995; erin@foliodesign .com; *foliodesign.com*.

Cabinetry—Downsview Kitchens; *downsviewkitchens.com*. **Cabinet installation**—GSR Woodworks; 619/733-5607. **Cabinetry hardware**—RK International; *rkintl.com*. **Millwork**—Bates Building Company; *batesbuild .com*. **Backsplash and countertop** Hanstone Strato 2cm—Hyundai L&C USA; *hyundailncusa.com*. **Wire mesh for cabinetry glass**—Brass Grilles UK through Coverscreen; *coverscreen-shop .co.uk*. **Brass shelf hardware**—Brassworks; *brassrails.com*. **Fabric for banquette** Pebbled in Stormy—HBF Textiles; *hbftextiles.com*. **Upholsterer for banquette**—Quickstitch Upholstery; 619/448-6825. **Faucets**—Waterstone Faucets; *waterstoneco.com*. **Barstools** Chi Bar Stool in Brushed Gold Base—Nuevo; *nuevoliving.com*. **Dining chairs** Evelina Side Chair—Euro Style; *euro .style*. **Pendants above island** Camden Lantern in Natural Brass—Regina Andrew; *reginaandrew.com*. **Pendant above table** Swell LED Pendant—Design Within Reach; *dwr.com*. **Wood flooring** Heirloom Collection in Cardiff—Provenza; *provenzafloors.com*.

CAPE COD CHARMER

Pages 40–45

Architecture and design: Jenn Sanborn, ASID, Sacris Design, Amesbury, Massachusetts; Instagram @sacrisdesign; *sacrisdesign.com*.

Wall paint White Dove OC-17, **trim, ceiling, and perimeter cabinetry paint** Brick House Tan CW-145, **island paint** Black 2132-10, **paint for chairs** Rich Coral 028—Benjamin Moore; *benjaminmoore.com*. **Cabinetry** recessed flat-panel double Shaker style—Advanced Custom Cabinets; *advancedcustomcabinets.com*. **Cabinetry hardware** dark bronze and antique brass—Horton Brasses; *horton-brasses.com*. **Countertop stone and sink backsplash** Taj Mahal

Leathered Finish, **countertop stone in pantry** Tuscan Mist Leathered—Montes Marble & Granite; *montesmarble.com.* **Sink—**NBI Drainboards; *nbidbs.com.* **Faucet and water dispenser—**Kingston Kitchen and Bath; *kingstonbrass.com.* **Refrigerator** Sub-Zero, **island cooktop and ovens** Wolf—Sub-Zero Group; *subzero-wolf.com.* **Dishwasher—**Miele; *mieleusa.com.* **Sconces in kitchen, pendants over sink—**Hudson Valley Lighting; *hudsonvalleylighting.hvlgroup.com.* **Sconces and chandelier in dining area—**Visual Comfort through Circa Lighting; *circalighting.com.* **Table in dining area** custom—Keystone Ridge Designs; *keystonerdigedesigns.com.* **Painted chairs** custom—Sika-Design; *sika-design.com.* **Seat cushion fabric for chairs** custom Rollo in Denim—InsideOut Performance Fabrics; *insideoutperformancefabrics.com.* **Seat cushion trim for chairs** custom Saisions in Terra—Samuel & Sons; *samuelandsons.com.* **Skirt fabric in pantry** custom—Mr. & Mrs. Howard for Sherrill Furniture; *sherrillfurniture.com.* **Natural woven shades—**Alta Window Fashions; *altawindowfashions.ca.* **Hand-knotted wool rug under table—**homeowner's collection. **Hand-knotted wool runners in kitchen—**Jaipur Living; *jaipurliving.com.*

RUSTIC & REFINED

Pages 46–51

Interior design: Ginger Barber, Ginger Barber Interior Design, 2025 West Alabama St., Houston, TX 77098; 713/523-1925; ginger@gingerbarber.com; *gingerbarber.com.*

Builder: John Dreiss, (formerly with) Purple Sage Construction, Galveston, Texas.

Cabinetry hardware window sash pull—Rocky Mountain Hardware, **plumbing and hardware fixtures—**Westheimer Plumbing & Hardware; *westheimerplumbing.com.* **Island cabinet, French duck decoys above cabinets** antiques—MAI Memorial Antiques & Interiors; *maihouston.com.* **Countertops—**Caesarstone; *caesarstoneus.com.* **Pewter tiles—**Material Bespoke Stone + Tile; *materials-marketing.com.* **Range and microwave** Wolf, **wine cooler** Sub-Zero—Sub-Zero Group; *subzero-wolf.com.* **Dishwasher—**Bosch Home Appliances; *bosch-home.com.* **Faucets** Perrin & Rowe Georgian Era Bridge Kitchen Faucet with Sidespray, **bar faucet** Perrin & Rowe Georgian Era Single Hole Bar/Food Prep Faucet, **kitchen sink** Shaws Original Fireclay Farmhouse Apron-Front Sink—House of Rohl; *houseofrohl.com.* **Woven shades—**Hunter Douglas; *hunterdouglas.com.* **Pendant lights—**Circa Lighting; *circalighting.com.* **Barstools—**Minton-Spidell; *minton-spidell.com.* **Bread basket, tian bowl—**Ginger Barber Interior Design; *gingerbarber.com.* **Rugs—**Creative Flooring Resources; *creativeflooringresources.com.*

GOOD AS GOLD

Pages 52–57

Interior design: Jana Erwin and Audrey Tehauno, Nest Design Group, Houston; 281/898-8579; nest.designs@icloud.com; *nestinteriordesigngroup.com.*

Builder: Philip Robbins, Bentley Custom Homes, 5233 Bellaire, Suite B-310, Bellaire, TX 77401; 713/592-0180; philip@bentleycustomhomes.com; *bentleycustomhomes.com.*

Cabinetry custom—Bentley Custom Homes; *bentleycustomhomes.com.* **Cabinetry hardware—**Restoration Hardware; *rh.com.* **Countertops—**Mont Blanc quartzite. **Backsplash tile** custom hand-painted terra-cotta by Tabarka—Architectural Design Resources; 713/877-8366. **Iron shelving—**Ross Metal Works; *rossmetalworks.com.* **Range** Wolf, **refrigerator** Sub-Zero—Sub-Zero Group; *subzero-wolf.com.* **Range hood** Venetian plaster finish—Jay P. Iarussi; Instagram @jayiarussi. **Faucet** unlacquered brass finish by Rohl, **sink** fireclay by Maidstone—Elegant Additions; *elegantadditions.net.* **Island pendants** Goodman Medium Hanging Light by Visual Comfort—M & M Lighting; *mmlighting.com.* **Windows—**Jeld-Wen; *jeld-wen.com.* **Blue dishes on shelves—**Target Stores; *target.com.* **Stools** Cornelia Leather Stool—Ballard Designs; *ballarddesigns.com.*

SMOOTH BLEND

Pages 58–63

Architecture: GTH Architects, 105 Revere Drive, Suite F2, Northbrook, IL 60062; 847/715-9395; info@gtharchitects.com; *gtharchitects.com.*

Interior design: Rebekah Zaveloff, KitchenLab Interiors, Chicago, Michigan, Miami, Colorado, California; 773/495-4557; info@kitchenlabinteriors.com; *kitchenlabinteriors.com.*

Builder: John Carey, JC Custom Home Builders, Elmhurst, Illinois; 630/816-7662; jccustomhomebuilders@gmail.com.

Cabinetry—custom rift-cut white oak. **Stain for cabinetry—**custom. **Paint for cabinetry** White Dove OC-17—Benjamin Moore; *benjaminmoore.com.* **Cabinet hardware** Massey Hardware Collection—Rejuvenation; *rejuvenation.com.* **Countertops** Bianca Perla quartzite, **backsplash behind range** porcelain Laminam—Marble & Granite Supply of Illinois; *marble-granites.com.* **Tile—**Tabarka Studio; *tabarkastudio.com.* **Appliances** Sub-Zero—Sub-Zero Group; *subzero-wolf.com.* **Pendant lights in kitchen, breakfast nook lighting—**

RESOURCES

Circa Lighting; *circalighting.com.* **Sconces at window**—Schoolhouse; *schoolhouse.com.* **Faucets** Taft—Newport Brass; *newportbrass.com.* **Island table**—Selamat Designs; *selamatdesigns.com.* **Island chairs** vintage by McGuire Furniture—Chairish; *chairish.com.* **Breakfast nook table** vintage burlwood, **breakfast nook chairs** vintage—Chairish; *chairish.com.* **Banquette**—Arhaus; *arhaus.com.* **Fabric for banquette** Ipanema—S.Harris through Fabricut; *fabricut.com.* **Rug** vintage—High Point Market; *highpointmarket.org.*

FAMILY TIES

Pages 64–69

Architecture: Brad Lewis, William D. Schwarz, Paige K. Richards, Schwarz Lewis Design Group, 1550 Spring Rd., Suite 100, Oak Brook, IL 60523; 630/537-1416; blewis@schwarzlewis.com; *schwarzlewis.com.* **Design:** Julie Zich, Julie Zich Interiors, 4947 Woodland Ave., Western Springs, IL 60558; 708/955-8158; juliezichinteriors@gmail.com; Instagram @juliezichinteriors; *juliezichinteriors.com.* **Wall paint for breakfast room** Normandy 2129-40—Benjamin Moore; *benjaminmoore.com.* **Millwork throughout**—Trimax Woodworking and Cabinetry; *trimaxwoodworkingandcabinetry.com.* **White cabinetry, walnut cabinetry with brass trim, range hood**—Julie Zich Interiors; *juliezichinteriors.com.* **Cabinet fabrication**—Kenrose Kitchen Cabinets; 217/543-3595. **Brass overlay fabrication**—Metal One; *metal1kc.com.* **Cabinetry hardware** brass—Myoh America; *myohamerica.com.* **Countertop** Leather Marble—MSI; *msisurfaces.com.* **Pantry countertop** Bella Blanco Quartz—Vicostone; *vicostone.com.* **Tile for range wall and inside black cabinets** custom—Century Mosaic; *centurymosaic.com.* **Range** Wolf—Sub-Zero Group; *subzero-wolf .com.* **Refrigerator, freezer**—Thermador; *thermador.com.* **Microwave**—Sharp; *sharpusa.com.* **Hood fabrication**—Custom Copper Hoods; *metalventhoods.com.* **Warming drawer near coffee bar**—Dacor; *dacor .com.* **Steam oven and coffee maker at coffee bar**—Miele; *mieleusa.com.* **Sink under window**—Kohler; *us.kohler.com.* **Sink in island**—De Giulio for Kallista; *kallista.com.* **Sink fixtures, pot filler faucet**—Newport Brass; *newportbrass .com.* **Pantry sink and sink fixtures**—Kohler; *us.kohler.com.* **Table at banquette**—custom. **Cushion fabric for banquette bench** Genslar 115—Kravet; *kravet.com.* **Bench fabricator**—Nelson Upholstery; 708/479-2626. **Table and bench in breakfast room, chairs at rounded banquette** Ballroom Side Chair in 4312-32 Linen by Hickory Chair—Walter E. Smithe; *smithe.com.* **Chairs in breakfast room**—Kindel Furniture; *kindelfurniture.com.* **Chair fabric in breakfast room** Henley Stripe Paper—Romo; *romo.com.* **Library light fixture at dark wood cabinetry** Woodbury Picture Light in Aged Brass by Hudson Valley Lighting—Lightology; *lightology.com.* **Sconces on range wall**—Hudson Valley Lighting; *hudsonvalleylighting.hvlgroup.com.* **Hanging light fixtures over island** San Marco Round Chandelier in Antiqued Brass—Restoration Hardware; *rh.com.* **Light fixture over breakfast room table**—Visual Comfort through Circa Lighting; *circalighting.com.* **Pantry light fixture**—Savoy House; *savoyhouse.com.* **Rug near island** custom—Rug Makers; *rugmakersinc.com.* **Rug near pantry**—HomeGoods; *homegoods.com.*

LIGHT TOUCH

Pages 70–75

Design: Martha O'Hara, Martha O'Hara Interiors, Minneapolis, 952/908-3150 and Austin, 512/222-3201; design@oharainteriors.com; *oharainteriors.com.* **Wall paint** Blue Veil 875—Benjamin Moore; *benjaminmoore.com.* **Cabinet paint** Alabaster SW 7008—Sherwin-Williams; *sherwin-williams.com.* **Countertop and backsplash** Calacatta Valentin—MSI Surfaces; *msisurfaces .com.* **Cabinet knobs** Eden in Honey Bronze, **cabinet and appliance pulls** Brixton in Honey Bronze—Top Knobs; *topknobs.com.* **Sink** apron-front sink with low smart-divide—Kohler; *us.kohler .com.* **Kitchen faucet** pullout spray in Brilliance Luxe Gold, **faucet for bar** single hole—Brizo; *brizo.com.* **Double ovens** 30-inch wall oven, **refrigerator** 48-inch panel-ready side-by-side, **dishwasher** panel-ready—KitchenAid; *kitchenaid.com.* **Range** 43-inch in Blanc—La Cornue; *lacornueusa.com.* **Hood insert**—Warners' Stellian; *warnersstellian.com.* **Pendants over island** rustic white finish, **sconces over window** hand-rubbed antique brass finish with linen shades—Visual Comfort through Circa Lighting; *circalighting .com.* **Counter stools** rattan in natural finish—Sika Design; *sikadesignusa.com.* **Runner** vintage Millie Turkish, **rug in front of bar** vintage Prudence Oushak—Fay + Belle; *fayandbellerugs.com.* **Flooring** refinished walnut flooring with custom stain—original to home. **Cookbooks, cutting boards, handmade utensil holder, large basket**—Gray Home + Lifestyle; *grayhomeandlifestyle.com.* **Pastel art** vintage—Clarabel Vintage & Antiques; *clarabelvintage.com.*

SURFACE APPEAL

Pages 76–79

Interior design: Caren Rideau, Kitchen Design Group, 15415 Sunset Blvd., Suite 106, Pacific Palisades, CA 90272; 310/454-6447; caren@kitchendesigngroup.com; *kitchendesigngroup.com.*
Interior design: Bonesteel Trout Hall, Pacific Palisades, CA 90272; 310/454-8762; hello@bonesteeltrouthall.com; *bonesteeltrouthall.com.*
Cabinetry custom—Kitchen Design Group; *kitchendesigngroup.com.* **Marble and tile flooring** Calacatta—Arizona Tile; *arizonatile.com.* **Paint on tub riser** Light Blue No. 22—Farrow & Ball; *farrow-ball.com.* **Plumbing fixtures—**Horus; *horusfrance.com.* **Light fixtures—**The Urban Electric Co.; *urbanelectric.com.* **Medicine cabinets—**Restoration Hardware; *rh.com.*

NATURALLY MODERN

Pages 80–83

Architecture: Robert Coyle, Coyle Design Group, 23183 La Cadena Dr., Suite 101, Laguna Hills, CA 92653; 949/677-2484; robert@dezign-group.com.
Interior design: Leigh Lincoln and Aly Morford, Pure Salt Interiors, 881 W. 16th St., Newport Beach, CA 92663; 949/314-3286; leigh@puresaltinteriors.com; *puresaltinteriors.com.*
Builder: Rick Forehan, (formerly with) Forehan Construction, San Juan Capistrano, CA; *forehanconstruction.com.*
Cabinetry, built-in shelving, and linen cabinet—Custom Cabinets by Jeffrey Elsenpeter; 714/315-3031. **Countertops—**Marbolis; *marbolis.com.* **Hardware—**Schoolhouse; *schoolhouse .com.* **Vanity backsplash—**Tabarka Studio; *tabarkastudio.com.* **Shower wall tile—**Bedrosians Tile & Stone; *bedrosians.com.* **Shower floor tile—**Mission Tile West; *missiontilewest.com.* **Bathtub, showerhead, faucets—**House of Rohl; *houseofrohl.com.* **Toilet—**Icera; *icerabath.com.* **Mirrors** custom—Best Framing; *bestframing.com.* **Vanity lighting—**Lostine; *lostine.com.* **Window treatments—**Sole Shades; *soleshades.com.* **Flooring—**Bravada Hardwood; *bravadahardwood.com.* **Vanity bath mats** Mackenzie Kilim Rug, **towels—**Pure Salt Interiors; *shoppe.puresaltinteriors.com.*

HOLLYWOOD HEYDAY

Pages 84–87

Architecture: Ryan Street, Ryan Street Architects, 2414 Exposition Blvd., Suite B-140, Austin, TX 78703; 512/421-0800; info@ryanstreet.com; Instagram @ryanstreetarchitects; *ryanstreet.com.*
Interior design: Nancy Bulhon and Julia B. Collins, Bulhon Design Associates, Austin; 512/476-2785; interiors@bulhon .com; *bulhon.com.*
Wall paint Ammonite No. 274—Farrow & Ball; *farrow-ball.com.* **Cabinetry hardware—**Alexander Marchant; *alexandermarchant.com.* **Sinks** POP undercounter sink by American Standard, **sink faucets and tub filler** Avanti by Rohl, **tub** Coastal Freestanding by American Standard—Ferguson; *ferguson.com.* **Floor tile** Snow White marble, **countertops** Calacatta Borghini marble—Decorum Architectural Stone; *decorumstone.com.* **Accent marble tile insert** Calacatta Mosaic by Artistic Tile—Architectural Tile & Stone; *architecturaltilestone.com.* **Mirror** custom—Bulhon Design Associates; *bulhon.com.* **Sconces** Laura—Visual Comfort through Circa Lighting; *circalighting.com.* **Windows** Lincoln—Centex Sash & Door LP; *centexsashanddoor.com.* **Vanity chair, rug—**homeowners' collection.

SIMPLE SPLENDOR

Pages 88–91

Architecture: W. Travis Mattingly, Architectural Solutions, Inc., Houston; 713/973-6989; tmattingly@asi-design .com; Instagram @design.asi; *asi-design.com.*
Interior designers: Alexandria Elam and Paige Murphy, Alex Interiors, 4910 Candletree Drive, Houston, TX 77018; 832/390-9664; alex@alexinteriorsinc.com; *alexinteriorsinc.com.*
Builder: Thompson Custom Homes, 1414 Woodvine Drive, Houston, TX 77055; 832/327-0197; help@thompsoncustomhomes.com; *thompsoncustomhomes.com.*
Wall paint Custom Plaster Greek Villa SW 7551—Sherwin-Williams; *sherwin-williams.com.* **Countertops** Turkish Pasha marble—QTS; *masonrycare.com.* **Shower tile** Rue Pierre Blanc antique marble—Walker Zanger; *walkerzanger.com.* **Shower fixtures, vanity faucet and bathtub** Horus French plumbing, **tub filler, cabinet hardware—**Fixtures & Fittings; *fixturesfittings.com.* **Flooring** Atlas Beige limestone—Exquisite Surfaces; *xsurfaces .com.* **Armoire** early 20th century French Biblioteque—Joyce Horn Antiques; *joycehornantiques.com.* **Chandelier** Culp Associates—Dennis & Leen; *dennisandleen.com.* **Fabric shade** Kerry Joyce, **grass shade** Hartman Forbes—Topstitch; *topstitchdrapery.com.* **Sconces—**Circa Lighting; *circalighting .com.* **Mirror above sink vanity—**Provenance Antiques; *provenance antiquesatlanta.com.* **Makeup vanity mirror—**Glamcor; *glamcor.com.* **Makeup vanity stool—**homeowner's collection.

Finishing

TOUCHES

> "MARBLE PATINAS AND UNLACQUERED BRASS WILL AGE AND GET BETTER WITH TIME."
>
> —CATHY POSHUSTA, HOMEOWNER AND DESIGNER

Beautiful Kitchens & Baths™ (ISSN 2157-3972), Spring 2023. *Beautiful Kitchens & Baths* is published twice a year in February and May by Meredith Operations Corp., 1716 Locust St., Des Moines, IA 50309-3023.

PHOTO *John Granen* STYLIST *Janna Lufkin*

Made in United States
North Haven, CT
20 July 2023

39280790R00055